MSRI Mathematical C

MW01255158

Math Circle
by the Bay

**Topics for
Grades 1–5**

Laura Givental
Maria Nemirovskaya
Ilya Zakharevich

MSRI
Mathematical Sciences Research Institute
Berkeley, California

AMS AMERICAN
MATHEMATICAL
SOCIETY
Providence, Rhode Island

This volume is published with the generous support of the Simons Foundation and Tom Leighton and Bonnie Berger Leighton.

2010 *Mathematics Subject Classification.* Primary 00A05, 00A07, 00A08, 00A09, 97-01, 97A20, 97A80, 97D50, 97E40, 97E50.

For additional information and updates on this book, visit
www.ams.org/bookpages/mcl-21

Library of Congress Cataloging-in-Publication Data

Names: Givental, Laura, 1958– author. | Nemirovskaya, Maria, 1972– author. | Zakharevich, Ilya, 1962– author. | Mathematical Sciences Research Institute (Berkeley, Calif.)
Title: Math circle by the bay: Topics for grades 1–5 / Laura Givental, Maria Nemirovskaya, Ilya Zakharevich.
Description: Providence, Rhode Island: American Mathematical Society, [2018] | Series: MSRI mathematical circles library; 21 | "MSRI, Mathematical Sciences Research Institute, Berkeley, California." | Includes bibliographical references and index.
Identifiers: LCCN 2018025745 | ISBN 9781470447854 (alk. paper)
Subjects: LCSH: Mathematics–Study and teaching (Elementary) | Mathematics–Study and teaching (Elementary)–California. | Mathematics–Study and teaching (Elementary)–Activity programs. | Games in mathematics education. | AMS: General – General and miscellaneous specific topics – Problem books. msc | General – General and miscellaneous specific topics – Recreational mathematics. msc | General – General and miscellaneous specific topics – Popularization of mathematics. msc | Mathematics education – Instructional exposition (textbooks, tutorial papers, etc.). msc | Mathematics education – General, mathematics and education – Recreational mathematics, games. msc | Mathematics education – General, mathematics and education – Popularization of mathematics. msc | Mathematics education – Education and instruction in mathematics – Teaching problem solving and heuristic strategies. msc | Mathematics education – Foundations of mathematics – Language of mathematics. msc | Mathematics education – Foundations of mathematics – Reasoning and proving in the mathematics classroom. msc
Classification: LCC QA13.5.C2 G58 2018 | DDC 372.7–dc23
LC record available at https://lccn.loc.gov/2018025745

In memory of Marina Ratner

Contents

Preface

Who the target audience of this book is

This book is intended for people who are already running a math circle or are thinking about organizing one. It can be used by parents to help their motivated math-loving kids or by elementary school teachers. We also hope that very bright fourth or fifth graders will be able to read this book on their own.

What math circles are

For about a century math circles blossomed in Eastern Europe. Twenty years ago they began to proliferate throughout the United States.

There are so many different flavors and approaches to math circles that it would be impossible to give any definition of what a math circle is. For us the defining common feature of all math circles is that interaction between the students is a significant driving force of the meetings, encouraging kids to learn from each other.

What makes this book special

The main features of this book are the logical sequence of the problems, the description of class reactions, and the leading questions or hints given to kids when they get stuck. This book tries to keep a balance between two goals: inspire readers to invent their own original approaches, while being detailed enough to work as a fallback in case the teacher needs to prepare a lesson on a short notice.

Who we are and how this book came about

Until about 10 years ago math circles were almost exclusively limited to middle and high school students. There was a widespread belief among math circle organizers (including the authors) that math circles do not make a lot of sense until the age of 12.

In Berkeley, the ice was broken in the fall of 2009 when Natasha Rozhkovskaya, while visiting MSRI, gathered a group of about 30 kids, grades 1–3, at UC Berkeley. The program was a huge success, creating an enormous demand for similar programs. The program continued to grow at UC Berkeley after Natasha's departure and then spread to other locations.

This book is based on selected topics we taught in math circles for elementary school students at UC Berkeley, Stanford, Dominican University (Marin County, CA), and the University of Oregon (Eugene).

Our programs enroll over 500 kids each year, with many still remaining on the waiting lists. There is no real selection process and the children are split into two age groups: grades 1–2 and 3–4 (or 2–3 and 4–5 in the Eugene math circle). Weekly sessions are 50–55 minutes long, with 25–30 students (and two instructors) per group. Being closely connected to the University of Oregon, the Eugene Math Circle is an exception: a number of undergraduates work as assistants so that there is approximately one instructor per six students, thus allowing more one-on-one time. In the case of a smaller teacher/student ratio we write very detailed class notes and require the parents to go over them with their kids as a part of the homework. This allows us to have significantly deeper discussions in the class.

How we select our topics

For classes we try to choose topics with deep mathematical context, which are parts of a continuously developing stream of mathematical thought. These topics are just as engaging and entertaining to the children as typical "recreational math" problems, but they can be developed deeper and to more advanced levels.

Our goal is to come up with a theme that will be exciting for first graders and can be taught to fourth graders, and later to middle schoolers, high schoolers, undergrads, graduate students, professors, and so on. There are naturally arising connections between such themes, which provide opportunities even for the young students to see how rich the interplay of math concepts can be.

While Olympiad-style problems are very important tools that attract many kids into math by challenging them, we do not need these tools. Our approach is to keep kids interested by presenting mathematics as a particular way to explore the world. We use Olympiad-style problems only occasionally as warmups and challenges.

As time goes by, we continue to learn how to present more and more advanced topics in our classes. Some of the themes we cover now were not imaginable even a couple of years ago. When immersed in a certain topic, the children comprehend surprisingly advanced material at amazing depth, allowing them to solve very challenging problems.

Since we enjoy coming up with new themes, we have enough to almost never repeat the same topic to the same kids.

How we teach

To hold the kids' attention and to fuel their enthusiasm, we vary the pace and topics by interlacing the main theme with warmup problems, discussion of the homework, and occasionally hands-on projects. We also spice up the presentation of the main topic by calling kids to the board, engaging them in dialogues, and encouraging independent problem solving. Occasionally we give an introductory warmup problem a week or two before starting an in-depth discussion of a new theme to let the material sink in. Warmups also help to cope with late arrivals. We keep a stack of challenging problems for the kids who are ahead of the rest of the class.

It is very important to balance two conflicting requirements: making problem statements unambiguous for the children and at the same time easy to understand. Presenting problems as funny or even silly stories excites the kids and keeps them engaged. Most of our problems have names or characters associated with them; when we later address such problems by these names, the kids easily recall them. We always have a bag of manipulatives (little cubes, coins, sticks, etc.) for the young hands-on learners.

Quite a few kids need to overcome their fear of making a mistake. We help them by turning question-and-answer exchanges into playful dialogues where making a mistake is a part of the game. We tell the kids, "The best mathematicians make a lot of mistakes working on a problem; it is a part of the process. What is important is that they correct them later." Our students even came up with an inside joke: "I made a mistake. I am done with the first step of solving the problem."

Many kids struggle with verbalizing their ideas, even after successfully solving the problem. Moreover, some of them do not see what the point is in explaining their solution. We have to return to this again and again, asking the class to repeat or improve an already presented solution. This introduces students to the basics of precise mathematical discourse.

A few observations

We are often asked how to draw more girls into math circles and keep them involved. In our experience, it happens without any additional effort on our side. The girls typically start stronger and progress very well. More than that, we were told that the percentage of girls in the middle school math circle went up significantly since our elementary program had started.

Another surprising fact is that while we have almost no pre-selection of the children, our retention level is very high. Only a few kids drop out after a semester, and many stay until they grow out of our program, continuing to middle school, and later high-school levels of the math circle, which are run separately (and differently).

In many cases we cover the same material in grades 1–2 (2–3 for Eugene) as in grades 3–4 (4–5 for Eugene), although at a slower pace and in lesser depth. Surprisingly, if we take into account the amount of prior knowledge and stamina for sitting and focusing longer, the difference between the older and the younger groups is not that significant. The younger students digest information slower, and the older students retain it better; nevertheless, at times the younger classes proceed with the same speed as the older ones.

Structure of the book

Each of the first five chapters represents one of the larger themes. Material in Chapter 1 can be either a stand-alone topic or taught as a part of the other themes. The other four themes are mostly independent from each other and comparable in difficulty. From experience we know that all classes are different, so we do not believe it makes sense to estimate how much time a particular topic will take. However, we do not expect that these five themes can take any less than two years to cover.

The remaining chapter and section provide supplementary material. Chapter 6 contains selected warmups and challenging problems. As we have already mentioned, this chapter includes the problems to be given 1–2 weeks before a specific topic is introduced. At the end of the book is a short section containing handouts with biographies of the mathematicians mentioned in the book.

The notes for the teachers are marked by $\boxed{\textit{Teacher}}\!\!\!\!\!\!\rightarrow$. They provide practical insight and suggestions for math circle instructors on organizing classes.

"Math Context" notes give more formal and sometimes more advanced context for the conclusions the students came to while working on the problems.

Acknowledgments

This book would have never appeared were it not for Zvezda Stankova and Natasha Rozhkovskaya. Zvezda Stankova, with her infinite energy, organized the original Berkeley Math Circle basing it mainly on real mathematical topics, as opposed to the preparation for Olympiads, common at the time. Natasha Rozhkovskaya, with her impeccable style of teaching, was the founder of the math circle for kids in elementary school.

We would like to thank Sergei Ovchinikov, one of the BMC Elementary organizers and one of the initial authors of this book, who then moved on to pursue other endeavors.

We would not be the teachers we are today without the forming influence of the books *Math from Three to Seven* by Alexander Zvonkin [1] and *Mathematical Omnibus* by Dmitry Fuchs and Sergei Tabachnikov [2], as well as discussions with Arkady Vaintrob.

We cannot imagine how it would be possible to teach without help from the Departments of Mathematics, Computer Science, and Economics at Berkeley, as well as the mathematics departments at Stanford and at the University of Oregon. They not only provided classrooms for math circle sessions but also gracefully put up with a lot of disturbance coming from our lovely but noisy students. In the case of the University of Oregon, this help included funding, providing undergraduate assistants, and basic logistics.

We are thankful to Jeffrey Musyt, Annie Zeidman-Karpinski, Lizka Vaintrob, Arkady Vaintrob, Dmitri Fuchs, Ira Kloumova, Michail Brin, Alisa Givental, Anna Polishchuk, Vera Serganova, Alexander Givental, Alexander Polishchuk, Sasha Shapiro, Elena Blanter, Elena Pavlovskaia, Vadim Matov, and Inna Zakharevich for reading the drafts of this book and giving us their very valuable comments.

Last, but not least, we would like to thank our families, who directly participated in teaching our math circles, coming up with ideas for the topics, and passionately helping us to survive the long and stressful process of writing this book.

Chapter 1

Numbers as Geometric Shapes

"Squares can be circular; I saw such a square in Paris," one child said in our class. The child meant Bastille square in Paris.

Teacher The material presented in this chapter is used in other chapters of the book.

Examples of Figurate Numbers

Numbers that can be presented as geometric shapes have been studied since ancient times, and are often called *figurate numbers*. A legend attributes figurate numbers to the ancient Greek philosopher and mathematician Pythagoras, who lived about 2,500 years ago.[1]

It is believed that his followers, the Pythagoreans, assigned magical properties to numbers which may be drawn as geometric shapes made of dots. Imagine, for example, constructing figurate numbers out of pebbles on the beach. You might represent 10 as a triangle, 16 as a square, and 15 as a rectangle.

Problem 1.1. Drawing Figurate Numbers. Represent the numbers 3, 6, 9, and 10 each as figurate numbers in more than one way.

The students came up with quite a few arrangements (shown below). They were excited to discover that 6 can be constructed as a rectangle (1×6 or 6×1 or 2×3 or 3×2), a hexagon, or a triangle. A couple of students found that 10 can be arranged into a three-dimensional tetrahedral pyramid.

---

[1]The handout with Pythagoras's biography can be found on page 165.

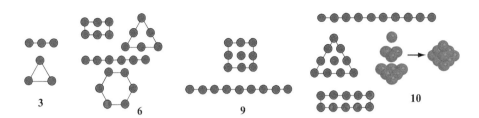

Surprisingly, no one noticed that the circular (polygonal) arrangement, similar to a hexagonal arrangement for 6, works for any other number. Linear arrangements work for any number too.   ◼

Square Numbers

A *square number* is the number of objects which may be arranged into a square shape. Such numbers are arguably the best-known examples of the figurate numbers, and most of our students have already heard about them.

What would be convenient to use instead of pebbles or balls to construct squares? The children proposed using square tiles, "Just use the grid squares in the notebook," they said.

Problem 1.2. Computing Squares. Draw 1-by-1, 2-by-2, 3-by-3, 4-by-4, and 5-by-5 squares. Count the number of tiles in each of them. Compute the number of tiles in the 20-by-20 square.

The students immediately drew the five squares shown below and found the number of tiles in each of them; 1, 4, 9, 16, and 25. Some did it by multiplication (for example, $3 \times 3 = 9$) and others by counting tiles in rows or columns (for example, $3 + 3 + 3 = 9$). A few children counted individual tiles around the sides of the squares and then inside in circular order, which was more error prone.

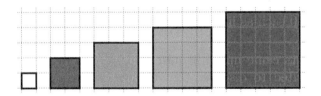

Many students familiar with multiplication computed the number of tiles in a 20-by-20 square as $20 \times 20 = 400$. Others found the answer by splitting the 20-by-20 square into four 10-by-10 pieces as shown below, $4 \times 100 = 400$. Some students couldn't find this approach on their own and required a hint: "Split the 20-by-20 square into parts that you know."

10×10 square	10×10 square
10×10 square	10×10 square

■

This is a good opportunity to introduce the students to the *power notation*. We like to tell the children that the mathematicians are "lazy in a good way" or "productively lazy": they want to do the work in the most efficient way possible. So, instead of writing $3 + 3 + 3 + 3 + 3$, they came up with a shortcut; we call it multiplication: $5 \times 3 = 15$.

Similarly, raising to a power is a shortcut for repeated multiplication:

$$2^4 = 2 \times 2 \times 2 \times 2 = 16.$$

In the notation 2^4, the number that is being multiplied (2) is called the *base*, and the number of times it is multiplied (4) is called the *exponent*.

As an example we computed $2^1 = 2$, $2^2 = 4$, and $2^3 = 8$. Several kids asked what is 2^0. The opinions of the students about what it should be were divided between it being 1 and it making no sense at all. Looking at a sequence 2^1, 2^2, 2^3, 2^4, ... we can see that each next number is obtained by doubling the previous one. After noticing that, by the same token, each previous number is a half of the next one, the students were able to conclude that 2^0 is a half of 2^1, that is, $2^0 = 1$.

Teacher ▶ In the discussion below we skip computing 7^2, 8^2, and 9^2 with the students who are not comfortable with the concept of multiplication.

Using the power notation, the children wrote down the first 10 square numbers: $1^2 = 1$, $2^2 = 4$, $3^2 = 9$, $4^2 = 16$, $5^2 = 25$, $6^2 = 36$, $7^2 = 49$, $8^2 = 64$, $9^2 = 81$, $10^2 = 100$.

Teacher ▶ It may be a good idea to give warmup Problem 6.1 before the next problem. It gives you a chance to discuss the meaning of the word "difference" beforehand. Finding the difference between two numbers, such as 5 and 3, not only provides the qualitative knowledge that 5 is greater than 3 but gives a quantitative result: 5 is bigger than 3 by 2. Similarly, subtracting two pictures gives a quantitative result, a picture of the difference.

Problem 1.3. Subtracting Squares. Draw and compute the differences (in whole tiles) between 1×1 and 2×2 squares; 2×2 and 3×3 squares; and 3×3 and 4×4 squares.

Everyone found that the difference between the first two squares is 3. However, a number of students didn't understand how to draw a picture for the difference and required a hint: "What will happen if you put a 1×1 square inside a 2×2 square?" Then everybody was able to draw the first picture:

The students explained that the 2×2 square has three additional tiles. In a few moments they came up with the remaining two pictures:

The 3×3 square has five tiles more than the 2×2, and the 4×4 square has seven tiles more than the 3×3 one.   ■

Problem 1.4. Sums of Consecutive Odd Numbers. Miles computed the sums $1 + 3$, $1 + 3 + 5$, and $1 + 3 + 5 + 7$ by arranging tiles into squares. He matched the colors of the tiles to the colors of the numbers. Reproduce his pictures. Compute $1 + 3 + 5 + 7 + 9 + 11 + 13$ using Miles's approach.

Many children asked for a hint: "Compute $1+3$, $1+3+5$, and $1+3+5+7$. Do you see a pattern?" Everyone noticed that these sums are consecutive squares: 4, 9, and 16.

Since $1+3 = 4$, the students decided to draw a 2×2 square for this sum. Surprisingly many students did not connect this problem with the previous one, and did not see what to do with the summands. Hint: "Color summands 1 and 3 in the square." As soon as one tile was colored, the students realized that the remaining three tiles represent the second summand — see the picture below on the left.

After that, the majority of the students quickly came up with the remaining pictures although a couple still needed a hint: "The picture for the sum $1 + 3$ helps color the picture for the sum $1 + 3 + 5$." In a few minutes everybody had the following:

In each of the above squares the summands are colored differently. One of these summands is a single tile and the rest are nested "L-shapes" (the name preferred by most kids) or "hooks". Pythagoreans called them *gnomons*.

To draw the sum $1 + 3 + 5 + 7 + 9 + 11 + 13$, the children added three more L-shapes to their picture for $1 + 3 + 5 + 7$ (the 4×4 square above on the right). They obtained the following 7×7 square:

So, $1 + 3 + 5 + 7 + 9 + 11 + 13 = 7^2 = 7 \times 7 = 49$.   ■

We asked, "Will any sum of consecutive odd numbers starting with 1 be a square?" The students replied, "Yes, just make a picture similar to the

7×7 square above." To make sure the students understood the concept we gave them the next few problems.

Problem 1.5. Find the Missing Number. How many odd numbers are in the sum: $1 + 3 + 5 + 7 + \cdots + ? + ?? = 11 \times 11$? Find the missing numbers: $?$ and $??$. Using the fact $10 \times 10 = 100$, calculate the sum (without multiplying 11 by 11 and without adding all odd numbers).

A few students were able to find the answers to this problem without drawing any pictures; instead they imagined the whole process in their heads.

A majority of the students drew the 11×11 square and marked the summands as a single tile and 10 nested L-shapes. Everyone noticed that each L-shape adds one tile to the side of the square. So, there are 11 odd numbers in the sum.

A couple of kids used the picture to calculate the number of tiles in the last two summands. A few others wrote down the first 11 odd numbers and found the missing summands this way. We asked them: "Do you want to use these methods for finding the last summand in the sum $1 + 3 + \cdots + ?? = 123 \times 123$? Find an approach which works even for bigger numbers." Soon the students realized that the missing number $??$ is the largest L-shape built on the 10×10 square. Typically, the students subdivide this L-shape into the top part (of length 11) and the rest (of height 10). We suggested a more symmetric and easier to handle way: subdivide it into the corner tile and two legs of length 10:

Thus, $?? = 10 + 1 + 10 = 21$. When we write a similar sum such as $20 + 1 + 20$ later, the students easily associate this with an L-shape.

The children proposed two approaches for finding $?$. Some of them counted the number of tiles in the second largest L-shape. It can be split into the corner tile and two legs of length 9, so, $? = 9 + 1 + 9 = 19$. Others noticed that $?$ is the odd number preceding 21. Therefore $? = 21 - 2 = 19$.

Since the difference between the 11×11 and 10×10 squares was already computed as the number of tiles in the largest L-shape, $11 \times 11 = 10 \times 10 + 21 = 121$.   ∎

Teacher ▷ It is a good idea to give the students a couple more similar problems. For example, "Calculate 12×12 without multiplication."

Problem 1.6. A Longer Sum of Odd Numbers. What square should Miles draw for the sum $1 + 3 + 5 + \cdots + 99$?

The students came up with two different ways to solve this problem.

Several kids figured out that the side of Miles's square equals the number of summands in the sum. Then they had to find how many odd numbers are between 1 and 99. A few determined kids wrote all the odd numbers from 1 to 99 and counted them. However, the majority noticed that every other number is odd. Some wanted to divide 99 by 2 and got stuck. Others decided to look at all numbers starting with 1 and realized that they can be split into pairs: odd, even. Number 99 is in the pair 99, 100. Then they counted the number of pairs from 1 to 100: $100 \div 2 = 50$. They found that there are 50 odd numbers from 1 to 99. So, Miles should draw a 50×50 square.

Other students decided that the sides of Miles's square can be computed from the largest L-shape that contains 99 tiles. Recalling the previous problem, the kids split this shape into the corner tile and two legs of length $98 \div 2 = 49$. So, the side of the L-shape is $49 + 1 = 50$, and Miles's square is 50×50. ∎

Problem 1.7. Triangular Tiles. How many green triangular tiles with 1-inch sides should be used to tile a red triangle with 2-inch sides? A blue triangle with 3-inch sides? A purple triangle with 4-inch sides? Find the pattern. Will the pattern continue forever?

The children started tiling the red triangle by placing three green tiles into its corners. One more tile fits in the place in the middle: ▲. To tile the blue triangle with 3-inch sides the kids placed the previous picture in its upper part. For this triangle they had no problem finding that the bottom strip requires five green tiles. Hence, it can be tiled with $4 + 5 = 9$ tiles.

Again, to tile the purple triangle with 4-inch sides, the kids placed the previous picture in its upper part. At this moment some students noticed a numerical pattern for the bottom strip: 1, 3, 5,... and quickly found out that seven green tiles will be needed. Others struggled to draw the bottom strip. Eventually, everybody found that the total number of tiles for this triangle is $9 + 7 = 16$.

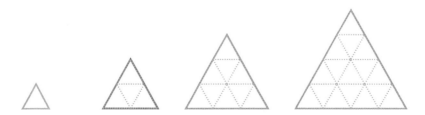

Thus, a square number of tiles is used each time. Why? Many students pointed out that by counting tiles row by row we obtain sums of consecutive odd numbers starting with 1. This is illustrated in the picture below.

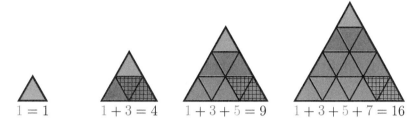

$$1 = 1 \qquad 1 + 3 = 4 \qquad 1 + 3 + 5 = 9 \qquad 1 + 3 + 5 + 7 = 16$$

How can we explain that this pattern will continue forever? The children noticed that with every step we add an additional row of tiles to the previous picture. That additional row contains two more tiles than the previous row (see shaded rhombi in the pictures above). So, indeed we get consecutive odd numbers. We already know that a sum of consecutive odd numbers starting with 1 is a square. ∎

Teacher We revisit this problem in Problem 1.18 and Problem 5.7.

Rectangular Arrangements

Any number of tiles can be arranged as a rectangle, and for most numbers this can be done in many ways. For example, five tiles can be arranged into a rectangle of width 1 and height 5 (a 1×5 rectangle on the left below) or into rectangle of width 5 and height 1 (a 5×1 rectangle on the right below):

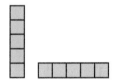

The children objected: "The second arrangement is the first one turned on its side." We agreed, but explained that for the next few problems we want to count them as two different arrangements.

We can arrange four tiles into three rectangles: 1×4, 4×1, and a 2×2 square (a square is also a rectangle).

We asked, "How many rectangular arrangements are there for six tiles?" — "Four," replied the kids.

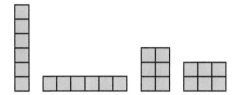

Problem 1.8. Rectangular Arrangements for 1 to 16 Tiles. For every number of tiles between 1 and 16, find the number of all possible rectangular arrangements and fill in the table below.

Tiles	1	2	3	4	5	6	7	8	9	10	11	12	13	14	15	16
Rectangles																

For every cell in the table the students wrote down or drew all the possible rectangles. Even the kids who did not know multiplication and division did it without much difficulty:

Tiles	1	2	3	4	5	6	7	8	9	10	11	12	13	14	15	16
Rectangles	1	2	2	3	2	4	2	4	3	4	2	6	2	4	4	5

An inspection of the table above leads to several interesting observations.

Problem 1.9. Only One Rectangular Arrangement. The students noticed that only one number has one rectangular arrangement: 1. Why?

Any number of tiles can be arranged into a rectangle of width 1. This rectangle may "fall" as shown below. In case of two or more tiles the "fallen" arrangement will differ from the initial one.

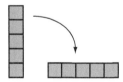

So for two or more tiles there are at least two rectangular arrangements. For one tile there is obviously only one rectangular arrangement. ■

Teacher ▶ Before posing the next problem we recall that one of the definitions of even numbers is that they can be divided into pairs. We discuss even and odd numbers in detail in Chapter 3, "Fibonacci Numbers".

Problem 1.10. Odd and Even Numbers of Rectangular Arrangements. When is the count of rectangular arrangements odd? Even? Explain.

The class noticed right away that only square numbers have an odd number of rectangular arrangements. They explained that if the number of tiles is a square, one rectangular arrangement will look exactly the same before and after the "fall". All other possible rectangular arrangements go in pairs: the width and the height may be switched (one before and one after the "fall").

That means that for square numbers the count of rectangular arrangements is odd; for the other numbers it is even. ∎

What numbers of tiles have exactly two rectangular arrangements? The students inspected the table and found these examples: 2, 3, 5, 7, 11, and 13. Such numbers are called *prime numbers*.

We asked, "What are the next two prime numbers?" —"17 and 19."

To give a more commonly used definition of prime numbers we need to introduce the word *divisor* (or *factor*). When a whole number is divided into equal groups, then both the number of the groups and the size of the groups are called divisors (or factors) of this number.

There are two ways to associate a divisor with a rectangular arrangement, by height and by width. The students did not see right away that the number of rectangular arrangements is always equal to the number of divisors. We hinted, "Look at the width only." For any number of tiles all of its rectangular arrangements have different widths, so counting divisors is the same as counting the rectangular arrangements.

Teacher ▷ This question doesn't arise when the rectangular arrangements are drawn in the order of increasing width. However, we chose an order of arrangements that helps with more difficult problems.

So, prime numbers are numbers that have exactly two divisors (or two factors); these divisors must be 1 and itself. The first prime number is 2, and it is the only even prime number. We asked the children, "Why?" The children explained that any other even number is at least divisible by 1, 2, and itself; therefore it is not a prime.

Problem 1.11. Exactly Three Rectangular Arrangements. When does a number have exactly three rectangular arrangements? Explain.

The class remembered that only square numbers have an odd number of rectangular arrangement or factors. Most of the children needed to write a few larger square numbers and compute the number of their arrangements (or factors) before they noticed the pattern:

Tiles	1	4	9	16	25	36	49	64
Rectangles	1	3	3	5	3	9	3	7

By looking at this table some students realized that 4, 9, 25, and 49 are squares of prime numbers, while 1, 16, 36, and 64 are squares of numbers that are not prime. A number of students did not make this observation and needed a hint: "Recall that $4 = 2^2$, $9 = 3^2$, $25 = 5^2$, and so on." If that hint was insufficient we gave another: "Squares of what numbers have three rectangular arrangements?"

The students argued that any square number other than 1 has at least three rectangular arrangements: of width 1, of height 1, and the square. Most of the students could not proceed further without our help. We asked the class, "Let's look at the square arrangement with side divisible by 3, but not equal to 3. Its tiles can be rearranged into two rectangles of width 1 and of height 1. Can you rearrange its tiles into a different rectangle?" The children suggested to split the square as shown:

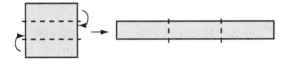

The height of each layer on the left and the rectangular arrangement on the right is greater than 1. So we found the 4th rectangular arrangement.

Even after discussing this example, the majority of the kids needed another prompt, "What if the side of the square is divisible by 5, but not equal to 5?" Finally, the children realized that if the side of the square is not a prime, it can be split in the same way as it was done above. For this problem we did not require more detailed explanation.

Moreover, we told the children that to finish the argument we need to understand why a square of a prime number cannot have more than three divisors (1, itself, and this prime number). This explanation is not elementary since it is based on the uniqueness of prime decomposition, which, in turn, relies on Euclid's algorithm.   ∎

Teacher While all of our students know that multiplication is commutative, most of them couldn't explain it on their own. Hence, we gave them the following problem.

Problem 1.12. Multiplication Is Commutative. Explain why $3 \times 5 = 5 \times 3$ without calculating the result. This explanation should work for other numbers too.

Teacher We prefer not to use the word "proof" and use the word "explanation" instead, until children prove a few facts by themselves and understand the concept. This concept is discussed later in Chapter 5, "Area".

The class immediately answered: "Of course, they are both 15!" We had to remind the children that they did not need to calculate the result and we could ask the same question about bigger numbers, for instance: "Is $98765 \times 54321 = 54321 \times 98765$?" We definitely want to skip these tedious computations.

Most of the children remembered that the above identity is called the *commutative property of multiplication*. They thought that giving the name for this property was sufficient for a solution. However, mathematicians always verify properties before using them — which is exactly what we do in math circles.

First, it is important to understand that the fact that the commutative law holds is *not obvious*. Since multiplication is just a shortcut for repeated addition, we can rewrite $3 \times 5 = 5 \times 3$ as $5 + 5 + 5 = 3 + 3 + 3 + 3 + 3$. In this form the students could see that this identity is not obvious anymore.

The majority of the students drew pictures similar to those on the left below. The number of tiles in the left rectangle is 3×5, and the number of tiles in the right rectangle is 5×3. The left rectangle turns into the right one after the "fall". Which means they have the same number of tiles. Hence, $3 \times 5 = 5 \times 3$.

Several kids came up with the different picture shown on the right. They argued that the dots arranged in a rectangle can be counted either row-by-row $(5 + 5 + 5)$ or column-by-column $(3 + 3 + 3 + 3 + 3)$. The total is always the same.

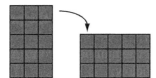   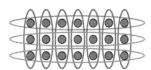

Triangular Numbers

Let us arrange coins into a triangular shape with all sides having five coins:

A few kids remarked that this picture is similar to a rack in pool.

Problem 1.13. Computing Small Triangular Numbers.
- Draw similar triangular arrangements of coins with up to six coins on the side.
- Propose a recipe for getting a bigger triangle from the previous one.
- Using this recipe fill out the empty cells in the table below.

Side		2	3	4	5	6	7	8	9	10
Coins, total										

The majority of students quickly drew triangles with sides 2, 3, 4, 5, and 6:

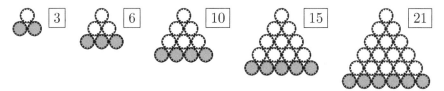

Even though we emphasized that each triangle has equal sides, a couple of kids made mistakes by putting three coins into the second row. To correct them we asked: "Does your triangle have equal sides?"

Additionally, the students started to argue about whether the triangle with side 1 should be drawn. We postponed this discussion until later.

The students immediately suggested a recipe for getting a bigger triangle: add one more row on the bottom of the previous triangle. While this answers the question, we pretended to be a robot, a technique we like to use when we want to get precise instructions. This robot was satisfied when the kids stated that the added row is one longer than the side of the previous triangle. Then the robot colored the added row.

First the majority of the students computed the number of coins in small triangles row by row, by calculating the sums below:

$$\mathbf{3} = 1 + 2,$$
$$\mathbf{6} = 1 + 2 + 3,$$
$$\mathbf{10} = 1 + 2 + 3 + 4,$$
$$\mathbf{15} = 1 + 2 + 3 + 4 + 5,$$
$$\mathbf{21} = 1 + 2 + 3 + 4 + 5 + 6.$$

Pretty soon the students noticed the shortcut: in every sum the yellow part can be replaced by the previous sum (the black number on the left). The students used this newly found shortcut to compute the number of coins for bigger triangles. This is shown by green arrows in the table.

Side	0	1	2	3	4	5	6	7	8	9	10
Triangular number	0	1	3	6	10	15	21	28	36	45	55

$$+1 \quad +2 \quad +3 \quad +4 \quad +5 \quad +6 \quad +7 \quad +8 \quad +9 \quad +10$$

While examining the table for bigger triangles the kids decided to include 0 and 1 by following the arrows in the above table in reverse. Though one coin does not look like a triangle, nobody had doubts how to make a triangular arrangement with side 1. The kids were excited to discuss an arrangement with side 0. ∎

The numbers obtained in the table above are called *triangular numbers*. For the sake of simplicity we call the number of coins in the triangle with side 2 the second triangular number, etc.

We asked the class, "Why did we draw pictures with triangular numbers using coins even though we used square tiles before?" The children explained that it is easier to pack round coins into triangles than the square tiles.

Problem 1.14. Computing the 13th Triangular Number. Using the table above compute the 13th triangular number.

We were surprised when a few students found the answer by taking the last computed triangular number, 55 (for side 10), and adding 13 to it. They were corrected by others: to use the shortcut from the previous problem one needs to know all intermediate triangular numbers. So, the answer is $55 + 11 + 12 + 13 = 91$. ■

Sometimes it is more convenient to visualize triangular numbers as right triangles. It can be done by bulldozing disks as shown below:

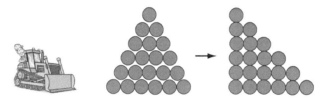

As an introduction to the next problem we computed a few sums of two consecutive triangular numbers. We let the kids discover that those sums were square numbers: $6 + 10 = 16$, $10 + 15 = 25$, etc.

Teacher The table with previously calculated triangular numbers should be erased before posing the next problems.

Problem 1.15. Sum of Two Consecutive Triangular Numbers. Jack drew a straight line splitting a 6×6 square made from coins into two triangular arrangements. What line did he draw and how many coins are in these triangles? How can Jack's discovery help to calculate the sum of the 9th and 10th triangular numbers? Note that you do not need to calculate these numbers separately.

A couple of kids ignored part of the conditions and drew a vertical line splitting the square into two rectangles. So, we gave a hint: "What line splits a square □ into two triangles?" The children knew that such a line is one of the diagonals of a square. In Jack's square the diagonal is made out of coins, which cannot be cut. Most of the students realized that one of the triangles must contain the whole diagonal. The side of that triangle is equal to the side of the square. So Jack's picture should be similar to the one below. The 6×6 square is split into triangles with sides 5 and 6.

    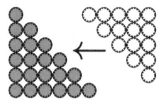

Looking at Jack's picture many children suggested replacing the triangle with sides 6 (shown in blue) by a triangle with sides 10, and replacing the triangle with sides 5 (shown in yellow) by a triangle with sides 9. This transforms the original square into the 10×10 square. A couple of students needed to draw the sum of two smaller triangular numbers (for example, the 3rd and 4th) to figure out the solution.   ∎

Problem 1.16. Make a Square. Find two ways to complete this picture to a square arrangement of coins.

This problem was solved interactively on the board in no time:

                                                                        ∎

Problem 1.17. Computing Triangular Numbers. Jill found a way to join the two triangles below into a rectangular arrangement. What are the sides of this rectangle? How does Jill's discovery help to calculate the triangular number for side 10?

Many children started by adding more coins, forming a square similar to the first square in the previous problem. Then they noticed that an extra column is needed to get the triangles of the right size. The result was a 4×5 rectangle. Only a couple of kids needed a hint for the first part of the problem: "The triangles may be rotated."

At this point we asked the class: "How does this picture help Jill compute the 4th triangular number? Propose a method that works for the 10th triangular number as well." The majority of the kids observed that the rectangle is made of two identical triangles. Hence, the 4th triangular number contains half of the coins used to make the rectangle: $4 \times 5 \div 2$.

While some kids finished the problem on their own, for others it was a challenge to imagine how the larger triangles fit together. We suggested considering triangles with side 5. The kids enlarged the blue triangle with sides 4 by adding an extra row as shown:

Then the children transformed the yellow triangle with sides 4 into a triangle with sides 5 by adding another column (or row). Looking at the resulting picture, the students calculated the 5th triangular number as a half of the coins in a 5×6 rectangle: $5 \times 6 \div 2 = 15$.

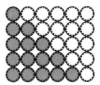

To compute the 10th triangular number the children had to figure out what rectangle would be obtained by putting together two triangles with sides 10 without a picture. It was not difficult: everybody realized that one side of the rectangle should be the same as the side of the triangle and the other bigger by 1. Hence, the 10th triangular number is $10 \times 11 \div 2 = 55$. ■

Problem 1.18. Count Triangular Tiles Again. Molly needs to find the number of small triangular tiles in the picture on the left. Waving her wand Terry the Fairy colored the picture as shown on the right. How did it help Molly?

The students immediately observed that the blue tiles form a triangular arrangement with sides 4. It took them longer to notice that the yellow tiles form a triangular arrangement with sides 3. Hence, the total number of tiles is the sum of two consecutive triangular numbers, the 3rd and the 4th. We already know that this sum is $4^2 = 4 \times 4 = 16$. ■

Will this method work for other triangles made out of triangular tiles? The children could see that a triangle with sides of any size can be colored yellow and blue similarly to the coloring above. The tiles of the same color form a triangular arrangement. The kids claimed that the side of the arrangement made from yellow tiles is one less than the side of the triangle made of blue tiles. Some explained it by pointing out that the yellow rows are between the blue rows. Others said that shifting yellow tiles up covers all the blue tiles except for the last row. Therefore, the total count of tiles in yellow and blue triangles is a sum of two consecutive triangular numbers. This sum is a square with side equal to the side of the larger triangle.

Several students recalled that the same result was obtained differently in Problem 1.7.

Quick Summations

Before introducing the next problem we tell the students about the life of Carl Friedrich Gauss (1777–1855), a great German mathematician and physical scientist.[2]

There is a well-known story about Gauss when he was almost 10 years old. According to the story, a teacher in Gauss's arithmetic class gave his students the mundane, tedious task of adding the whole numbers from 1 to 100. However, the teacher didn't get the long break he was looking for because young Carl solved it in a couple of minutes. And Gauss was the only one who got the correct answer.

Teacher ▸ We gave one of the two versions of warmup Problem 6.3 a couple of weeks prior to the following problem.

Problem 1.19. Sum of 1 to 100. Find the sum: $1 + 2 + \cdots + 99 + 100$.

Several students recognized that the sum is the 100th triangular number, and should be $(100 \times 101) \div 2 = 5050$.

A number of kids found the same sum by adding 1 and 99, 2 and 98, and so on, up to 49 and 51. So they got one hundred 49 times. Then, they added the last 100 and the leftover 50 and got the same answer as everybody else.

Others found the sum by grouping numbers 1 and 100, 2 and 99, 3 and 98, and so on. The sum of numbers in each group is 101 and there are 50 such groups. So, the sum is $50 \times 101 = 5050$.

One more group of kids wrote the sum twice as shown below:

$$
\begin{array}{ccccccccc}
& 1 & + & 2 & + & \cdots & + & 99 & + & 100 \\
+ & 100 & + & 99 & + & \cdots & + & 2 & + & 1.
\end{array}
$$

Then they added numbers in columns and got:

$$101 \ + \ 101 \ + \ \cdots \ + \ 101 \ + \ 101;$$

---

[2]The handout with Gauss's short biography can be found on page 166.

There are 100 terms, and the total is $101 \times 100 = 10100$. The answer is $10100 \div 2 = 5050$. ∎

People who usually tell the story about young Gauss think it paints a portrait of a very smart child. Apparently they never visited an Elementary Math Circle; a lot of our kids can also come up with the same or similar ways of solving this problem. This story should be considered a "historical anecdote" and told by those who do not know how smart 8-year-olds can actually be.

Problem 1.20. Revisiting the Sum of Odd Numbers up to 100. Find the sum: $1 + 3 + 5 + 7 + 9 + \cdots + 97 + 99$ using one of the methods from the Gauss story.

To evaluate the sum, the children immediately decided to group together 1 and 99, 3 and 97, and so on up to 49 and 51. Each group is 100 and there are $50 \div 2 = 25$ such groups because there are 50 terms to add (as in Problem 1.5). So, the sum is $25 \times 100 = 2500$. ∎

Cubic Numbers

In this section we discuss large cubes made out of little cubic building blocks. All children are familiar with them. A *cubic number* (also called a cube when it cannot be confused with the shape) is the number of cubic building blocks that make up a larger cube. This cube has equal number of blocks in three directions: width, depth, and height. We call a cube with 10 building blocks on every edge a 10-by-10-by-10 cube. The first cubic number is 1: a cube built of a single cubic building block.

Teacher ▷ While discussing a square, one can use "a corner" instead of a vertex and "a side" instead of an edge. For a cube, the word "side" creates confusion (ambiguity): it can mean either an edge or a face. We often discuss with the students how important it is to use precise words when doing math. For the 3-D figures one must use the words "edge" and "face". In our class using the word "a corner" instead of a vertex does not cause confusion.

Observing the cube (we usually bring a cardboard model, a box of tiny cubes or a Rubik's cube to the class), the children discovered that a cube has six faces, eight vertices, and 12 edges. The edges were the hardest to compute: four at the bottom, four at the top, and four vertical.

Problem 1.21. Computing Cubic Numbers. How many building blocks are in a cube with the edges of length 3?

Teacher We intentionally do not use words 3-by-3-by-3 cube because some children use it to compute the answer without understanding the geometry of the cube.

A number of students had a hard time visualizing such a cube. We helped them by drawing the cube with edges of length 3 on the board:

Some of the children tried to compute the number of building blocks in the following way: they saw nine square tiles on each of six faces of the cube and decided that the answer should be $6 \times 9 = 54$. A couple of kids added the invisible building block in the middle and got 55.

To help the students see their mistake we suggested they use the same approach for a cube with sides 2. This cube has six faces, each with four square tiles (no invisible blocks). So, the answer should be $6 \times 4 = 24$. However, this time everybody noticed that the cube consists of two layers with four building blocks each. Hence, the answer is 8. Why did the previous method give an answer three times too large? The kids realized that 24 is not the count of building blocks, but the total count of visible faces of the blocks. Since in a 2-by-2-by-2 cube each block is a corner block, every block is counted three times.

Now, all children computed the number of blocks in a cube with sides 3 correctly by breaking it into three layers. Each layer is a 3-by-3 square and consists of $3 \times 3 = 3 + 3 + 3 = 9$ building blocks. Thus, the answer is $3 \times 9 = 9 + 9 + 9 = 27$.

A couple of students, who still struggled, needed manipulatives (a set of small wooden cubes). ∎

We reminded the children about the power notation and together wrote the first few cubic numbers:

$$1^3 = 1 \times 1 \times 1 = 1,$$
$$2^3 = 2 \times 2 \times 2 = 8,$$
$$3^3 = 3 \times 3 \times 3 = 27,$$
$$4^3 = 4 \times 4 \times 4 = 64.$$

Teacher It helps to show the students the Rubik's cube before giving them the next problem.

Problem 1.22. Painted Cube. A $3 \times 3 \times 3$ cube is built out of white cubic building blocks. It is painted red outside (including the bottom). If we break this cube into building blocks, how many of them would have three red faces, two red faces, one red face, or stay entirely white?

What if the large cube was $4 \times 4 \times 4$?

Most of the children quickly noticed that the building blocks at the vertices of the large cube have three red faces and there are eight of them (the same number as vertices). Six building blocks have one face painted red: these blocks are located in the center of each face of the large cube. The children described the blocks with two red faces as blocks "in the middle of every edge of the large cube". Since there are 12 edges, there are 12 such blocks. Some of the children missed an entirely white cube. Hint: "What is the total number of cubes we just found?" It is $6 + 12 + 8 = 26$, but the $3 \times 3 \times 3$ cube consists of 27 building blocks. Finally, the students realized that there is a white building block in the center of the large cube.

Moving to the $4 \times 4 \times 4$ cube, it took children some time to find $6 \times 4 = 24$ building blocks with one red face (four in the middle of each of six faces of the big cube), $12 \times 2 = 24$ building blocks with two red faces (two in the middle of each of 12 edges of the big cube), eight building blocks with three red faces (at each of eight vertices of the big cube), and eight white building blocks forming an invisible $2 \times 2 \times 2$ cube in the center of the large cube. Some students computed the number of white blocks as the difference between the number of all blocks and those having at least one face painted: $24 + 24 + 8 = 56$, $64 - 56 = 8$. We pointed out that the kids who used the first approach to calculate the number of white blocks can doublecheck their answers: "Were all the building blocks accounted for?" "Yes, 24+24+8+8=64!" ∎

Teacher ▷ Sometimes we give the students a similar problem about a cube with only five, rather than six, painted faces.

Problem 1.23. A Cheese Cube and a Mouse. A 10-by-10-by-10 cube is made out of cubic cheese building blocks. Every night a little math-loving mouse eats the outermost layer of blocks (all the outside blocks including the bottom ones). For how many nights will it have food? How many cheese blocks will it eat each night?

Teacher ▷ The second part of this problem takes a lot of time and works well as homework.

Many students quickly realized that it will take the mouse five nights to finish the cube since the edges of the cube decrease by 2 every night: $10 \div 2 = 5$. Others required a hint: "Imagine the top view of the big cube. How would it look before and after the first night?" Some kids imagined the answer, others drew it:

Computing the number of small cheese cubes eaten on the first night was harder and we heard a variety of wrong answers, starting with 600: "There are six faces, 100 cubes each."

A number of students computed the correct answer directly. First, they removed the top and the bottom faces: $100 + 100$ blocks. On the remaining part of the outmost layer they noticed two 8-by-10 rectangles on the opposite faces. After removing those, two 8-by-8 squares remained. So, the total number of cubes is $2 \times 100 + 2 \times 8 \times 10 + 2 \times 8 \times 8 = 488$.

Only a couple of students realized that the number of blocks in the outer layer is the difference in block count of the large cube before and after the first night: $10 \times 10 \times 10 - 8 \times 8 \times 8 = 488$. However, as the children continued counting the number of building blocks eaten each night more and more of them discovered this approach: "Oh, it is so much easier than I thought!" The final results are shown in the table:

Night	1	2	3	4	5
Cube	$10 \times 10 \times 10$	$8 \times 8 \times 8$	$6 \times 6 \times 6$	$4 \times 4 \times 4$	$2 \times 2 \times 2$ · $0 \times 0 \times 0$
Number of blocks	1000	512	216	64	8 · 0
Eaten this night	488	296	152	56	8

Most students do not see the connection between the last two problems by themselves, and so we prompt them: "Look at the number 56 in the table. We have seen it recently in another problem. Where? What is the connection between these two problems?" In the "Painted cube" problem there were 56 painted blocks. They make up the outer layer.

Pyramids

Problem 1.24. Tetrahedral Numbers. Count the number of balls in the following triangular (tetrahedral) pyramid:

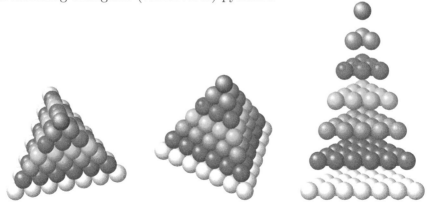

Note: We do not color the balls or include the picture on the right in the problem statement.

Some students began this problem by counting balls on four faces: $4 \times 28 = 112$; here 28 is the triangular number for side 7. Hint: "How many times did you count the top ball?" The kids realized that they counted each corner ball three times, repeating the same mistake as in Problem 1.21. Many realized that the number of balls in the pyramid should be counted layer by layer. The handout with the right picture shown above worked as the final hint.

There are seven layers, and each layer is a triangular number. Adding from the top, the number of balls in the pyramid is $1+3+6+10+15+21+28 = 84$. ∎

The total number of balls in such a tetrahedral arrangement (triangular pyramid with equal edges) is also a figurate number, called a *tetrahedral number*. We helped the class to write the first 10 tetrahedral numbers on the board:

$$\begin{aligned}
\mathbf{1} &: \quad 1, \\
\mathbf{2} &: \quad 4 = 1 + 3, \\
\mathbf{3} &: \quad 10 = 1 + 3 + 6, \\
\mathbf{4} &: \quad 20 = 1 + 3 + 6 + 10, \\
\mathbf{5} &: \quad 35 = 1 + 3 + 6 + 10 + 15, \\
\mathbf{6} &: \quad 56 = 1 + 3 + 6 + 10 + 15 + 21, \\
\mathbf{7} &: \quad 84 = 1 + 3 + 6 + 10 + 15 + 21 + 28, \\
\mathbf{8} &: \quad 120 = 1 + 3 + 6 + 10 + 15 + 21 + 28 + 36, \\
\mathbf{9} &: \quad 165 = 1 + 3 + 6 + 10 + 15 + 21 + 28 + 36 + 45, \\
\mathbf{10} &: \quad 220 = 1 + 3 + 6 + 10 + 15 + 21 + 28 + 36 + 45 + 55.
\end{aligned}$$

Teacher ▷ Having the first few tetrahedral numbers on the board helps with the remaining problems in this section.

Problem 1.25. Mouse Pyramid. A triangular pyramid is made out of cheese balls. A little math-loving mouse comes and eats all the cheese balls on the outside, including the bottom. Every cheese ball in the pyramid is eaten. How high can this pyramid be?

Find all the possibilities.

The students had no doubts that pyramids of height 1 and 2 would disappear. A few children decided that they found all the possibilities. Hint: "Look at the picture of the disassembled pyramid from the previous problem." Now many students realized that all six balls in the third (from the top) layer could be eaten from the sides. They concluded that the pyramid with three layers would also disappear. In a couple of minutes several kids discovered that in the pyramid of height 4 the fourth layer is the bottom layer, and thus would be eaten too.

At that point many students decided that they were done with the problem and the answer is 4. We had to ask them, "Are you sure it is not 5?" Only then did the class realized that the solution is not finished yet. Most of the students could find a ball (in the fourth layer) that would not be eaten in the pyramid of height 5.

If the children had a problem visualizing the remaining ball in a pyramid of height 5, we asked them to color it in a handout with a disassembled pyramid.   ■

Problem 1.26. Big Mouse Pyramid. A triangular pyramid of height 8 is made out of cheese balls. A little math-loving mouse comes and eats all the cheese balls on the outside, including the bottom. What shape remains? What is the height of this shape? How many balls have been eaten?

Hint: "Give the students the picture shown below on the left and ask them to mark the remaining balls."

Many students saw that the arguments of the previous problem are still applicable: the top three layers, as well as the bottom layer, are going to be eaten. A few cheese balls would still remain in the four layers:

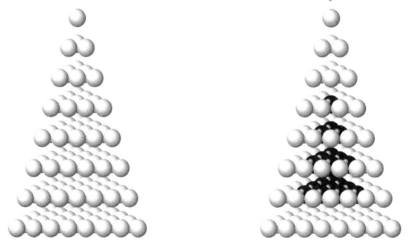

The students noticed that the remaining balls form a pyramid of height 4. This allowed them to find the number of eaten balls: there are 120 balls in the pyramid of height 8, and 20 in the pyramid of height 4; hence $100 = 120 - 20$ balls have been eaten.   ■

Problem 1.27. Huge Mouse Pyramid. A similar pyramid made out of cheese balls has 100 layers. Every night a little math-loving mouse eats all the balls on the outside (including the bottom ones). How many layers would remain after the first night? For how many nights will the mouse have food?

We were surprised when this problem turned out to be more difficult than we expected. While several students had a correct answer, most of the class had wrong answers spread between 50 and 99. The proposed correct arguments were the same as in the previous problem: since the picture of the top of the pyramid is the same (no matter what the pyramid's height is), the top three layers and the bottom layer would be eaten. So after the first night four layers would be completely eaten, and some balls would remain in the 96 layers.

Several students still had doubts about what would remain after the second night, but most of the class realized that four layers will be eaten every night, and arrived at the answer 92. Eventually the students figured out that it would take 25 nights to eat the whole cheese pyramid. ■

Problem 1.28. Square Pyramid. Count the number of balls in the square pyramid shown below on the left:

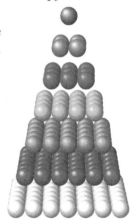

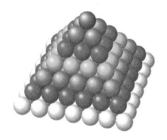

Teacher▸ We do not color the balls or include the picture on the right in the problem statement.

Some students tried to compute the number of balls by looking at the triangular faces and attempting to decompose the pyramid this way. We gave them a hint: "For which face is counting balls the easiest?"

Soon everybody deconstructed the pyramid into seven square layers as shown above on the right. Starting from the top, the total number of balls is: $1^2 + 2^2 + 3^2 + 4^2 + 5^2 + 6^2 + 7^2 = 140$. ■

Before discussing the next problem, we constructed the table with the first few tetrahedral and square pyramidal numbers on the board and asked the children, "What happens if we add two consecutive tetrahedral numbers?" After a few experiments, the students discovered that these sums are *square pyramidal numbers.*

Teacher▸ The next problem is the most challenging in this chapter. Many children struggled with visualization of three-dimensional shapes and required a lot of hints.

Problem 1.29. Splitting a Square Pyramid. Tetrahedral numbers for pyramids with three and four layers are 10 and 20. The total, $10 + 20 = 30$, is the number of balls in the square pyramid of height 4. Cheops claims that he can explain this observation by coloring some balls of the square pyramid. How did he do it?

The majority of the students required our help with finding a connection between the square pyramid and the tetrahedral pyramids. Hint: "Color the decomposed pyramid first." If that hint was insufficient, we gave another one: "Recall how each layer of the square pyramid is related to the layers of the tetrahedral pyramids." Many children remembered splitting a square into two triangles. So, they divided each layer of the decomposed square pyramid into two triangles coloring one of them. Assembling the colored layers produces the pyramid that can be split into the colored and uncolored parts. The uncolored part is the tetrahedral pyramid of height 4 and the colored one is the tetrahedral pyramid of height 3 as shown below.

The students claimed that the same method would work for any square pyramid.

Chapter 2

Combinatorics

Combinatorics is the art of counting. In this chapter we will count many things: colorings of bead chains, words of the Mumbo language, ice cream cones, walkways in Nowhere York city, friendly handshakes, and more. Somehow the answers to our exciting counting problems turn out to be boringly the same: either 10 or 45. This made one of our students remark:[1] "It looks like 45 is now the Answer to the Ultimate Question of Life, the Universe, and Everything." Hopefully, our discussions teach one to *foresee* why two different counting questions lead to the same result. Namely, the children can often establish a connection between different problems which guarantees the same answer even before the counting. Such a connection is called an *isomorphism*, a fancy term which the children love to use when they understand its meaning.

Teacher ▶ The familiarity with triangular numbers (in Chapter 1, "Numbers as Geometric Shapes") and with "off by one" situations (warmup Problems 6.4–6.9) comes in handy for the following material.

Coloring Beads

Problem 2.1. Coloring Two out of Five Beads. How many different 5-bead chains can you make by coloring two out of five beads and leaving the other three beads white?

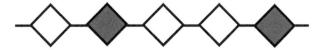

For this problem we give the class handouts with 12 copies of uncolored beads. After some trial and error many children managed to find the correct answer: 10. Others made inadvertent omissions or repetitions. Even the students who got 10 different chains were unable to explain why all the possibilities are exhausted. We pointed out this difficulty but postponed the actual discussion, giving the kids a chance to discover for themselves a systematic way of listing all choices. ■

---

[1] Apparently quoting "The Hitchhiker's Guide to the Galaxy" by D. Adams.

Problem 2.2. Coloring Three out of Five Beads. How many different 5-bead chains can you make by coloring three out of five beads blue?

Our students solved this problem almost immediately. They pointed out that particular colors do not matter: one can exchange blue and white beads in the previous problem. The answer is still the same, 10.   ∎

> **Math Context.** The equality of the answers to the last two problems is a particular case of the equality $\binom{n}{k} = \binom{n}{n-k}$. Here $\binom{n}{k}$ (read "n choose k") denotes the number of subsets of k elements in a set of n objects. This equality may be explained by replacing a subset of k elements by its complement consisting of $n - k$ elements. For example, instead of selecting seven objects out of nine, one can select the remaining two out of nine.

Teacher Our experience that the children realize right away that particular colors don't matter differs from Zwonkin's observations [1]. The most probable explanation is that he was working with much younger children.

Mumbo Language

Problem 2.3. Mumbo 5-Letter Words. The alphabet of the Mumbo people from Nowhere Land has only two letters, A and B. Every combination of these letters is a word. For example, BBB and ABA are Mumbo words. Find the number of Mumbo words with two As and three Bs.

Our students had the same difficulties as in the previous problem: repetitions, omissions, and no explanation why their answers are correct.

We suggested they come up with a system which would help to avoid repetitions and omissions. A few students proposed the list shown in the table below.

They started with placing the first letter A in the first spot and moving the second A through the remaining spots from left to right; then, placing the first letter A in the second spot, etc.

A	A	B	B	B
A	B	A	B	B
A	B	B	A	B
A	B	B	B	A

B	A	A	B	B
B	A	B	A	B
B	A	B	B	A

B	B	A	A	B
B	B	A	B	A

B	B	B	A	A

Now, the children were able to explain why the list has no repetitions or omissions: all the possible places for A are used. A couple of students commented that the words are listed in the same order as in a dictionary. They were excited to hear that they had discovered the method of ordering words which mathematicians call lexicographic or dictionary order, and which is indeed used in dictionaries.

In English only some arrangements of the 26 letters of the alphabet create meaningful words. For example, "hmett" is not a word. "Can one imagine a language with only two letters, and where any arrangement of these two letters makes sense?" It turns out that a language with a 2-letter alphabet is used in computers. The letters of this language are called "bits". We write them using digits 0 and 1. The name "bit" comes from "<u>BI</u>nary digi<u>T</u>". Any word in this language can be interpreted as a number.

Some children noticed that 10 was the answer to Problem 2.1, "Coloring Two out of Five Beads" as well. Is it a coincidence? We address this in Problem 2.6.

Ice Cream Cones

Problem 2.4. Four Ice Cream Flavors. Ann can put two scoops of ice cream in her cone side-by-side:

She must select two distinct flavors out of vanilla, chocolate, pistachio, and strawberry. How many different ice cream cones can she make?

Teacher ➤ Without the picture above many kids place the scoops one on top of the other, which makes chocolate-vanilla different from vanilla-chocolate.

We reminded our students that mathematicians are "lazy in a good way", and so they use shortcuts instead of writing long words, or drawing complicated pictures. The possible shortcuts for vanilla, chocolate, pistachio, and strawberry may be V, C, P, and S, respectively.

The children quickly realized that the choice CV (chocolate plus vanilla) is identical to VC (vanilla plus chocolate), and so on. Soon the children listed all possibilities making sure they are all different and none are omitted. Ann's choices were: VC, VS, VP, CS, CP, and SP. Thus, the answer is 6. ■

Problem 2.5. Five Ice Cream Flavors. What would happen if Ann had five flavors available? Now blueberry is added to the list of possible flavors.

This time a lot of students missed one or two combinations. Several children organized their solution in a systematic way, a few made a table. We added names for columns and rows in their table:

	V	C	S	P	B
V		VC	VS	VP	VB
C			CS	CP	CB
S				SP	SB
P					PB
B					

Students filled this table row by row. In the second row they left the cell CV empty since it is a duplicate of cell VC. Continuing this way one gets a triangular shape formed by 10 different ice cream combinations. The children immediately pointed out that 10 is a triangular number for side 4. A few students recalled that the answer to the previous problem was also a triangular number. Our children get very excited when they make such observations. ■

Math Context. The number $\binom{n}{2}$ ("n choose 2") is the number of pairs of objects in a set of n objects. Using the lexicographic ordering of pairs, it can be identified with the sum $(n-1) + (n-2) + \cdots + 2 + 1$, which is triangular number $T(n-1)$ for side $(n-1)$:

$$\binom{n}{2} = T(n-1) = \frac{n(n-1)}{2}.$$

Problem 2.6. Introducing Isomorphism. The answers to the three previous problems, "Coloring Two out of Five Beads", "Mumbo 5-Letter Words", and "Five Ice Cream Flavors", are the same. Is there a reason for this? What is the connection between these three problems?

We started by reminding the class of the systematic way of listing the Mumbo words. Then we gave the children the handout with uncolored beads and asked them to redo Problem 2.1 using the similar system.

Comparing the picture with the systematically colored beads and the table of the Mumbo words, the students noticed right away that they look alike. In a few moments someone suggested to write the letter A over the blue beads and the letter B over the white ones. Now the children were screaming, "The problems are the same!"

Comparing the problem of the colored beads with the problem of choosing two ice cream flavors turned out to be more difficult. Hint: "In the shop five containers with different flavors of ice cream stand in one line." Now, many students suggested that when Ann chooses two flavors, we should color the chosen containers blue. Then Ann's choices indeed look like colored beads!   ■

We told the children that sometimes two problems are related so that a solution to one of them can be translated into a solution for the other, and vice versa. Such problems are called *isomorphic*. We just discovered that all three problems, "Coloring Two out of Five Beads", "Mumbo 5-Letter Words", and "Five Ice Cream Flavors" are isomorphic.

Teacher ▷ Usually when we introduce mathematical terms in class we do not expect that the kids would remember them, and we refrain ourselves from using them in class. The word isomorphic is an exception: the students love this word and use it all the time.

Nowhere York City

Problem 2.7. Walks in Nowhere York. Andy's home and school in Nowhere York are shown below. Andy walks from home to school always choosing the shortest possible routes. Determine the number of such routes.

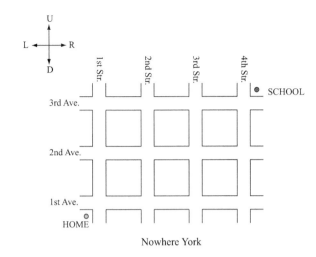

Nowhere York

To help the children to distinguish between left and right we mark the directions on the top of the picture.

First, we need to understand how the "shortest possible routes" look like. After some debate our students came to the conclusion that Andy should walk only right and up. Otherwise, the route would be longer, and one can make a shortcut as shown by the dashed line for the "red" route:

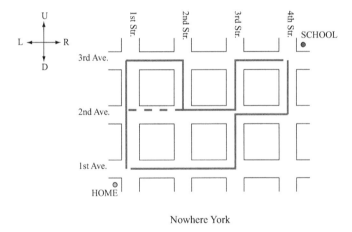

Nowhere York

Now, we can start drawing all possible routes from home to school. Initially, it was not obvious (at least to some of our younger students) that all the paths going right and up have the same length: all go three blocks right and two blocks up. Some made this discovery only after drawing a few paths. Also, one has to be careful not to repeat the same path, and it might be unclear why the drawings include all possible shortest routes, but, eventually, the students ended up with 10 different pictures.

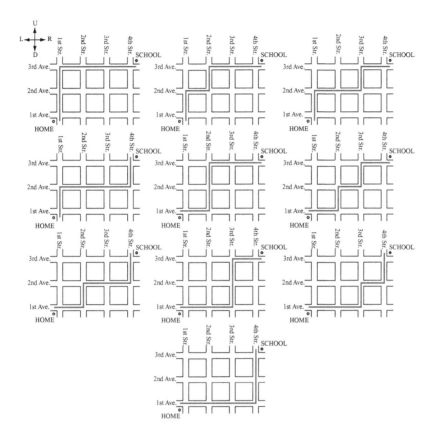

The children were excited to get the answer 10 again, and were sure that the problem should be isomorphic to each of the previous ones: "Coloring Two out of Five Beads", "Mumbo 5-Letter Words", and "Five Ice Cream Flavors". Some of the students were even able to find an explanation, the others needed a hint: "Record all possible shortest routes using the letter R for walking right and the letter U for walking up."

The 10 shortest paths are encoded by 5-letter words consisting of two Us and three Rs:

UURRR   URURR   URRUR   URRRU
RUURR   RURUR   RURRU
RRUUR   RRURU
RRRUU

Now, it becomes obvious that this problem is identical to the "Mumbo 5-Letter Words" problem: use A instead of U, and B instead of R. ■

The Handshake Problem

Problem 2.8. Handshakes of Five Friends. Five friends, Ann, Bob, Cal, Dean, and Eva, shook hands with each other. Each person shook hands with every other person once. How many handshakes occurred?

The best way to clarify what happens (especially to the younger students) is to ask five children to come to the board and shake hands with each other. We would like the children to find a systematic way to do this. The question: "Who will shake hands first?" is a good way to initiate the due process. Our students suggested that first Ann should shake hands with Bob, Cal, Dean, and Eva (four handshakes). Bob should be the next to shake hands. Since Bob already shook Ann's hand, he needs to shake hands only with Cal, Dean and Eva (three handshakes). Now comes Cal who shakes hands with Dean and Eva (two handshakes). Finally, Dean shakes hands with Eva (one handshake). Thus, the total number of handshakes is $4 + 3 + 2 + 1 = 10$, or the fourth triangular number.

Once again the students claimed that this problem must be the same as the ones we solved before. How can we find a connection between this problem and coloring of the beads?

Hint 1: "Let Ann, Bob, Cal, Dean, and Eva line up in a single row."

Hint 2: "Find a way to represent the handshakes between the two kids."

Our students proposed to color blue two kids shaking hands, for example, Bob and Eva:

Now the kids play the role of the beads. Different handshakes match different colorings of the beads. So the problems are isomorphic. The children were so pleased with their own idea that it took us a couple of minutes to calm them down. ∎

Problem 2.9. Handshakes of Six Friends. Six friends, Ann, Bob, Cal, Dean, Eva, and Fred, shook hands with each other. Each person shook hands with every other person once. How many handshakes occurred?

When we started discussing this problem the five kids who previously shook hands were still by the board. The kids suggested to invite one more child, Fred, to the board. They explained that the first five kids already shook hands with each other, so only Fred should shake hands with everybody else. Thus five more handshakes should be added to the previous answer; this may be written as $5 + 4 + 3 + 2 + 1 = 15$ handshakes, or the triangular number for side 5.

A couple of our students solved the handshake problems using a different approach. First, they counted how many times each of the six children shook hands. Each one shakes hands with everybody else, which means he or she shakes five hands. There are six children total, so the total number of handshakes is $6 \cdot 5 = 30$. "How come this answer is different (and wrong)?" Knowing the correct answer several students immediately realized that they had counted every handshake twice! For example, the Ann-Bob handshake was counted as Ann shaking Bob's hand and Bob shaking Ann's hand. To avoid double counting, the answer 30 should be divided by 2. ■

Sides and Diagonals

Problem 2.10. Connecting Dots. Five points A, B, C, D, and E are drawn in a circle. Tim connected every two points by a segment. How many segments did he draw?

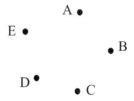

The students immediately identified the points with five friends shaking hands. The children explained that since the problems are "the same", the answers are also the same: there are 10 segments. ■

Same Problems with 10 Objects

Problem 2.11. Coloring Two out of 10 Beads. How many different 10-bead chains can you make by coloring two out of 10 beads blue?

The children unanimously agreed not to draw all the possibilities since there would be too many pictures for a 10-bead chain. Instead, they proposed to count the choices without drawing them.

First they looked at the 10-bead chains with the first bead colored blue. In this case there are nine choices for coloring the second bead blue: it can be any bead from the second through the tenth.

Then, if the first blue bead were in the second place, there would be only eight choices for coloring another bead blue. And so on.

The total number of different chains is $9+8+7+6+5+4+3+2+1 = 45$, the ninth triangular number. ■

Problem 2.12. Revisiting Mumbo Words and Handshakes. Invent a problem about Mumbo words that is the "same" as the "Coloring Two out of 10 Beads" problem.

Do the same for the handshake problem.

Teacher▷   This exercise emphasizes the idea of two problems being the same (being isomorphic). We needed to remind a couple of students the solutions to the Mumbo 5-letter word problem.

The children immediately proposed replacing the blue beads with As and the white beads with Bs. The new Mumbo problem would read as: "How many different words in Mumbo language are there with exactly two As and eight Bs?"

It was more challenging to formulate the handshake problem. Eventually the students remembered how they solved the handshake problem: they thought of kids as beads with two kids painted blue shaking hands. Since there are 10 beads in the chain now, there should be 10 children in the handshake problem. The students came up with the following: "Compute the total number of handshakes if ten friends want to shake hands with each other."   ■

Apples, Oranges, and More

Teacher▷   The following problems are more challenging. They should be done only if the students are comfortable with the problems in the previous sections.

Problem 2.13. Eight Apples for Three Kids. Find the number of ways to distribute eight apples between three children, Ann, Bob, and Cal. It is OK if somebody gets no apples at all.

Many students solved this problem by systematically considering all possibilities. To help them we drew the first two rows of the following table (where Ann has eight or seven apples) on the board:

Ann	Bob + Cal	Number of choices
8	0+0	1
7	0+1, 1+0	2
6	0+2, 1+1, 2+0	3
...	...	...
0	0+8, 1+7, ... 7+1, 8+0	9

If Ann gets eight apples, Bob and Cal both have none — only one choice. If Ann gets seven apples, one apple remains. It can go either to Bob or to Cal — two choices.

After filling the third row a number of children discovered the pattern 1, 2, 3 and continued it numerically. We insisted on the explanation for this pattern. Many kids noticed that if Bob's numbers are listed starting with 0 and ending with 8, there are $8 + 1 = 9$ numbers in total. Other children simply filled the table row by row, listing all possibilities. Everyone found that the total number of ways to distribute eight apples between Ann, Bob, and Cal is $1 + 2 + 3 + 4 + 5 + 6 + 7 + 8 + 9 = 45$.

By now the class was on the lookout for the problems with the same answers. They immediately suspected that this problem is "the same" as coloring 10 beads.

Teacher ▸ This isomorphism is more complicated than those considered before. In some of our classes we had to explain it to the students on the board.

A lot of children noticed that there are eight white beads in the chain and associated them with eight apples in the problem. Only one or two kids were able to figure out what the blue beads represent. The rest received a hint: "Every chain represents a way to divide the apples between the kids. Given the chain below, how do we divide apples?"

Soon the students came up with this explanation:

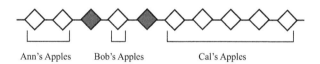

Ann's Apples   Bob's Apples   Cal's Apples

which may be translated into the "apple" language in the following way:

Several students had difficulties translating cases with two blue beads next to each other or with a blue bead at either end of the chain. In a few minutes the class found the answers. If the first bead is blue, Ann has no apples. If two blue beads are adjacent, Bob has no apples. If the last bead is blue, Cal has no apples.

Going back from apples to beads it is crucial to have apples and separators on an equal footing: eight apples plus two separators equals 10 total, which we translated into 10 beads (eight white and two blue). ■

Problem 2.14. Eleven Oranges for Three Kids. In how many ways can 11 oranges be given to Ann, Bob, and Cal if each child should get at least one orange?

Some of our students successfully solved this problem by going through the table, similar to the first solution to the previous problem. Some children, to our great pleasure, were trying to reduce this problem to the previous one. They discovered that if we start with giving Ann, Bob, and Cal one orange each, the remaining eight oranges may be divided in exactly the same manner as eight apples in the previous problem (when zero counts were allowed). So, the answer is 45.

A couple of students had no idea how to begin the problem and needed a hint: "We have three more oranges than we had apples in the previous problem, but now everybody must get at least one orange. How would you distribute the oranges?"

A couple of students solved the problem by constructing an unexpected direct isomorphism with the beads problem. They figured out how to fit 10 beads into the problem with 11 oranges. If the oranges are arranged in a line, there are 10 gaps between them and a bead can be placed in every gap:

The blue beads separate the oranges given to different kids, the remaining eight beads remain white. For example, if Ann gets four, Bob one, and Cal six oranges, the picture looks like this:

Even if blue beads were next to each other (or at the beginning, or at the end of the row), every child would get at least one orange. Now, removing the oranges, only a chain of beads remains:

So, each arrangement of two blue beads and eight white beads in a chain gives a way to divide oranges. This is the isomorphism!   ■

Problem 2.15. Nine Plums for Three Kids. In how many ways can nine plums be given to Ann, Bob, and Cal if Ann has to share one plum with her baby sister and must get one while the other kids don't mind getting none?

This problem was not difficult for the students. They suggested to give one plum to Ann first. The remaining eight plums should be divided in the same way as apples. Thus, the answer is 45.   ■

Problems about Numbers

Teacher ▶ Some of our students solved the next two problems by direct counting or by constructing an elaborate isomorphism with the coloring of 10 beads. Here we do not explain either of these solutions. Instead, we discuss the simpler isomorphisms with the problems from the previous section discovered by our students.

Problem 2.16. Sum of Digits Is 9. How many three-digit numbers with the sum of all digits being 9 are there?

A number of students solved this problem right away. The rest needed some hints: "How many digits are there? What are the options for the first digit of any three-digit number? What about other digits?" After realizing that the first digit must be at least 1, the children concluded that the problem is identical to the previous one, nine plums for three kids. The first digit is the number of Ann's plums, the other two digits represent Bob's and Cal's plums, so the answer is 45. ∎

Problem 2.17. Sum of Digits Is 11. How many three-digit numbers with all digits greater than zero and their sum being 11 are there?

Almost all children recognized that this problem is the same as 11 oranges for three kids: the first digit is Ann's oranges, the second is Bob's, and the third is Cal's oranges. Thus, the answer is 45 again. ∎

Problem 2.18. Decreasing Digits. How many eight-digit numbers are there, such that every digit is greater than the one on its right? 87543210 is an example of such a number.

Teacher ➤ This is an example of a problem where constructing the isomorphism is significantly easier than direct counting. To invent the direct counting one needs a system that tracks the missing digits instead of those present, but noticing this immediately leads to an isomorphism. So, we won't discuss the direct counting approach, which was used by a couple of our students.

Some of our students solved this problem very quickly by making the following discovery: any eight-digit number in which every digit is greater than the one on its right is obtained from the sequence 9 8 7 6 5 4 3 2 1 0 by erasing two digits. Let's think of the erased digits as the blue beads, and the remaining digits as the white beads. Then any coloring of two out of 10 beads blue corresponds to one of the numbers we are looking for. Thus, the problems are the same and the answer is 45. A few students struggled with this problem for a long time, and finished it at home. Here is a hint for them: "Consider a number that fits the requirements. Which digits, from 9 to 0, are missing?" ∎

Harder Problems

Teacher ➤ The following two problems are quite challenging and are intended for more advanced students.

Problem 2.19. Arranging Red and White Balls. In how many ways can nine red and eight white balls be arranged in a row with no two white balls next to each other?

This time all of our students were trying to see whether this problem was the same as coloring of a 10-bead chain. Some found the solution quickly but others struggled.

Hint 1: "Draw the red balls first."

Hint 2: "What is the largest number of white balls (instead of 8) that can be arranged without touching?"

The kids pointed out that nine red balls create 10 possible spots for the white balls. Eight out of 10 spots should be occupied by white balls — place them there. The remaining two spots are left empty. Placing blue beads there creates a familiar picture: coloring two out of 10 beads. Therefore, there are 45 ways to create the required arrangement.

Empty spots

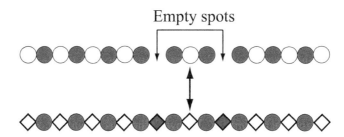

Problem 2.20. Ordering Ice Cream. An ice cream shop has nine flavors of ice cream. In how many ways can Sam order a two-scoop cone (see Problem 2.4) if he is allowed to choose the same flavor twice?

Many children solved this problem by directly counting all possible ways of choosing flavors. There are nine choices for the first of Sam's scoops, 1 through 9; let's list all of them in a table:

Flavor of the 1st scoop	Flavor of the 2nd scoop	Number of choices
1	1, 2, 3, ..., 9	9
2	2, 3, ..., 9	8
3	3, ..., 9	7
...	...	...
9	9	1

The first row of the table lists all combinations containing the 1st flavor. In the second row the 1st flavor is not an option for the 2nd scoop to avoid duplication (all the combinations with the first flavor are already in the first row). Continuing with the rows, the students obtained the sum $9 + 8 + 7 + 6 + 5 + 4 + 3 + 2 + 1 = 45$.

It looks like this problem is "the same" as coloring "Two out of 10 Beads". Why? The explanation happened to be truly challenging, and we had to help the students. After we drew nine ice cream containers in a row, one of our students came up with a good hint. She noticed that $8 = 9 - 1$, and it is the number of gaps between the containers. So, she put eight white beads in the gaps.

Where should one put two blue beads? After some pondering the children decided that the blue beads should mark the scoops that Sam chose. Now, ignoring the containers, but looking only at the beads, we obtained a ten-bead chain with eight white and two blue beads. This means that the problems are the same and have the same answer, 45.

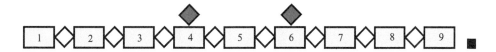

Chapter 3

Fibonacci Numbers

We asked our students to guess the next number in the following sequence:

$$1, \ 1, \ 2, \ 3, \ 5, \ 8, \ \ldots$$

One child suggested that the next number is 11 since the resulting sequence represents the ages of the siblings in her family.

Soon, the students found the actual rule: every number after the second one is the sum of the previous two numbers. This sequence is called the *Fibonacci sequence*.

Teacher ▷ To prepare for this chapter we had asked the students to guess the next number in a few sequences a couple of weeks earlier (see warmup Problem 6.10).

Building Strips with Squares and Dominoes

Problem 3.1. Squares and Dominoes. We have two kinds of building blocks: squares ▢ and dominoes ▭. Find the number of ways to build strips of length 1, 2, 3, 4, 5, and 6 out of these blocks.

Teacher ▷ Using colors helps the children to see the patterns and come up with the recursive relation faster.

With the children's help we got the following picture on the board for strips of length 1, 2, and 3:

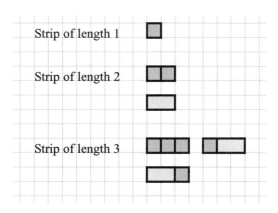

There is only one way to build a strip of length 1, two ways to build a strip of length 2, and three ways to build a strip of length 3.

We put these results into a table and asked, "How many ways are there to build a strip of length 4?"

Number of squares in a strip	1	2	3	4	5	6	7	8
Number of ways to build a strip	1	2	3					

Most students immediately yelled four, continuing the obvious numerical pattern. However, this guess turned out to be wrong, since in less than a minute some children found five different ways.

Teacher ▷ For the children this was a striking example of an obvious pattern that should have worked, but didn't. The breaking of such an obvious pattern justified the question: "Will this pattern continue forever?" which appears again and again in our discussions of patterns.

Soon the rest of the children also found five ways to build the strip of length 4, and we summarized the result on the board:

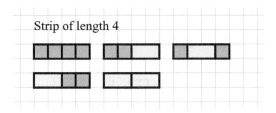

The strip of length 5 took more time. To ensure that all possible ways of building the strip are found and none are repeated, we reminded the students of how important it is to have a systematic way of listing the possibilities (problem "Mumbo 5-Letter Words", page 26). There are many ways to accomplish this; one of them helps to discover the recurrence relation. We led the class towards it: "The picture on the board follows a certain system. Can you figure this system out?"

Many students observed that in the top row the first building block is always a square, while in the bottom row it is always a domino. The same principle should work inside the strips: always place a square first; then, only if all arrangements starting with a square are already listed, use a domino. Some of the children still had difficulties drawing all possible arrangements, so we suggested denoting squares and dominoes with letters A and B. It allowed the children to follow a familiar dictionary order. Some of them even mentioned that the strips are arranged like the words in a dictionary (problem "Mumbo 5-Letter Words", page 27).

At last, everybody was able to produce the following pictures for the strip of length 5:

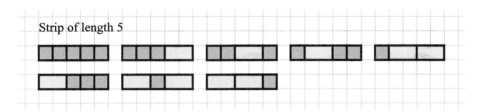

We added the latest results to the table:

Number of squares in a strip	1	2	3	4	5	6	7	8
Number of ways to build a strip	1	2	3	5	8			

At this point our students recognized the Fibonacci sequence discussed at the beginning of this chapter. The prediction for the number of ways to build a strip of length 6 was unanimous: $13 = 5 + 8$. We all agreed that checking this prediction by drawing so many arrangements would take a significant amount of time and is error prone. It might be easier to justify why the next number should always be a sum of the two previous numbers.

Teacher ▷ In many classes the children do not need such detailed hints, as described below. Based on our experience the following is the worst case scenario.

To explain this rule, let us consider the case we are already familiar with, the strip of length 5. Most of our students needed a hint: "What can be the first step in building the strip?" The children suggested to put a square first (for them, first means on the left). We asked, "How should we build the remaining part of the strip?" and covered the leftmost square in every strip in the top row:

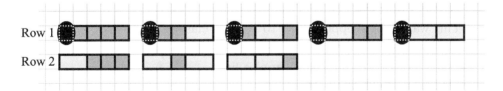

Now a few kids were able to proceed on their own. They recognized that the colors on the uncovered parts of the strips are the same as on the strips of length 4. Several kids still needed additional clues: "What is the length of the remaining part?"; "Do we know how to build the strip of length 4?"

The class concluded that if the first building block is a square, there are five ways to build it. This number is the same as the total number of ways to build the strip of length 4.

We asked the class, "Are we done yet?" Many kids exclaimed, "No, we should find what happens when the first building block is a domino, look at the bottom row!" They proposed to cover the leftmost domino in every strip of the bottom row:

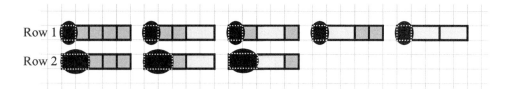

The kids discovered that the uncovered parts of the strips in the bottom row match three known strips of length 3. They got very excited and yelled, "This means that the pictures of strips of length 3 and 4 'are hidden' in the picture of strips of length 5!" Hence, there are $5 + 3 = 8$ ways to build the strip of length 5.

Finally, the students were able to come up with the following argument for the strip of length 6:

(1) If the left block of this strip is a square, the remaining part is the strip of length 5. We already know that there are eight ways to build the strip of length 5 with squares and dominoes.

(2) If the left block of this strip is a domino, the remaining part is the strip of length 4. We already know that there are five ways to build the strip of length 4 with squares and dominoes.

(3) We have no other choices for the leftmost block! The total number of ways to build the strip of length 6 is the sum: $5 + 8 = 13$.

One can apply the same approach to strips of length 7, 8, 9, ... This means that every number in the table above is the sum of the two previous numbers. It is the Fibonacci sequence! ∎

Teacher ▷ Our students cannot formulate statements which involve unknown quantities. So we did not ask them to state "a general argument". It is enough if they can see that "the same argument also works for longer strips."

This was a good opportunity to tell the class that what we did is very similar to the work done by real mathematicians.

- We studied the simplest examples first.
- We figured out the pattern.
- We invented a systematic way of reasoning.
- We came up with an argument that works for all cases: those we considered before, and all the others!

The children were very excited to hear this.

Parking Problems

Teacher ▷ Most children find the next two problems more challenging, although their solutions are the same as for the previous problem.

Problem 3.2. Parking Cars and Motorcycles. A parking lot has 10 narrow parking spaces in a row. A motorcycle takes one space, and a car takes two spaces. How many ways to park cars and motorcycles are there so that all the spaces are taken? What if there are 12 parking spaces in the parking lot? Note that all the cars look exactly the same and all the motorcycles look exactly the same too.

The class started drawing different parking arrangements but soon discovered that there are too many of them. Hint: "Solve a similar but simpler problem first. It will give you a clue for solving the more complex one." After drawing parking arrangements for lots of length 1, 2, 3, and 4, the children recognized the pictures, "This problem is the same as 'Squares and Dominoes'." The answers should be 89 and 233 — just continue the table from the previous problem. However, when we asked the students to explain why the problems are the same, many of them struggled. The following analogy proved helpful.

There are two languages, Blockian and Parkian. Blockian has only two words: "square" and "domino". Comparing the last two problems, can you translate these words into Parkian?

BLOCKIAN	PARKIAN
Square	?
Domino	?

In a few minutes the students figured out that a "square" should be a "motorcycle" and a "domino" should be a "car". This translation establishes a way to turn the strips of squares and dominoes into ways of parking motorcycles and cars. We can translate in both directions, which means the number of ways to build a strip must be the same as the number of ways to park. As we found earlier the Fibonacci sequence is the answer to Problem 3.1, "Squares and Dominoes"; therefore it is the answer for this problem too. Some children remembered that such problems are called isomorphic (page 29). ∎

Problem 3.3. Parking Cars Only. A parking lot has 10 narrow parking spaces in a row. Each car takes two spaces. How many ways are there to park cars in this parking lot if some parking spaces might remain empty? What if there are 12 parking spaces?

Unexpectedly, a few kids could not visualize parking arrangements with empty spaces. To help them we had to discuss a few examples, drawing them on the board.

As with the previous problem we suggested the children investigate shorter parking lots: "What if there are only two or three parking spots? Can you draw the possible parking arrangements?" Using this hint most of the children easily drew the pictures for lengths 2, 3, and 4, however some students omitted the case of a completely empty parking lot. When this mistake was noticed most of the class was able to explain how to turn this problem into the previous one: park a motorcycle in each empty space. Several students also suggested to translate the word "motorcycle" to "free space".

Thus, the answers to the problem are 89 and 233.   ■

Problem 3.4. Parking Cars and Motorcycles With Empty Spaces. A parking lot has seven narrow parking spaces in a row. A motorcycle takes one space, and a car takes two spaces. How many ways to park cars and motorcycles are there if some parking spaces might remain empty?

This problem is harder than the ones discussed before. Once again we advised our students to start with the simpler examples: parking lots with 1, 2, or 3 parking spaces. The results are shown below:

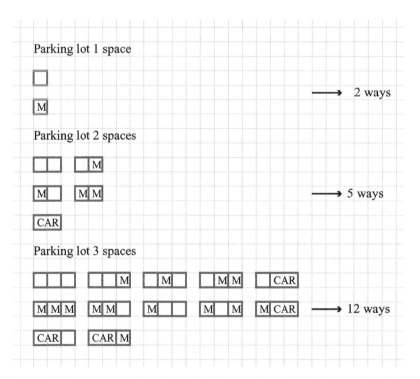

Many children remembered a similar system of listing strips in Problem 3.1, "Squares and Dominoes", and gave the following recipe:

- List all parking lots with the first space empty.
- Then list all the parking lots with a motorcycle in the first space.
- Then list all the parking lots where the car is parked in the first two spaces.

Several kids could proceed on their own, the rest needed our hint: "Why does the first row have five pictures, while the last row has two?" The hint helped and many children were able to explain what would happen with four parking spaces:

(1) If the first space is empty, what remains has three spaces. We already know that there are 12 ways to park in the parking lot with three spaces.

(2) If the first space is taken by a motorcycle, what remains has three spaces. Again, there are 12 ways to park in this case.

(3) Finally, if there is a car on the left, then what remains has two spots. As we saw there are five ways to park in these spots.

There are no other possibilities of what can be parked in the first spot. The total number of parking arrangements for the parking lot of size four is:

$$12 + 12 + 5 = 2 \times 12 + 5 = 29.$$

The same reasoning can be used for larger parking lots. Going from the parking lot with four spaces to a parking lot with five spaces, from the parking lot with five spaces to a parking lot with six spaces, and so on, the kids came up with the table:

Number of parking spots	1	2	3	4	5	6	7
Number of ways to park	2	5	12	29	70	169	408

Problem 3.5. Parking Cars, Motorcycles, and Trucks. A parking lot has 10 narrow parking spaces in a row. A motorcycle takes one space, a car takes two spaces, and a truck takes three spaces. How many ways to park cars, motorcycles, and trucks are there so that all the spaces are taken?

The class began the problem by looking at shorter parking lots. The children easily drew all possible parking arrangements for the parking lots of length 1, 2, and 3:

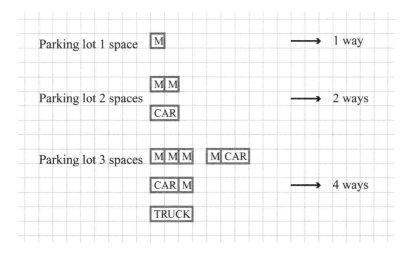

Then the students quickly came up with the solution for a parking lot with four spaces:

(1) If there is a motorcycle in the first spot, what remains has three spaces. As we saw there are four ways to park in these three spaces.

(2) If there is a car on the left, what remains has two spaces. We already know that there are two ways to park in these two spaces.

(3) If there is a truck on the left, what remains has one space. We already know that there is only one way to park in one space.

Since we listed all the possibilities for the type of vehicle at the left end, the total number of parking arrangements is $1 + 2 + 4 = 7$. Continuing in the same manner for longer parking lots, the kids filled the following table:

Number of parking spots	1	2	3	4	5	6	7	8	9	10
Number of ways to park	1	2	4	7	13	24	44	81	149	274

Counting Routes

This is yet another problem where the answer is a Fibonacci sequence.

Problem 3.6. Postman Rob. In a village, postman Rob always delivers mail going left-to-right horizontally or diagonally:

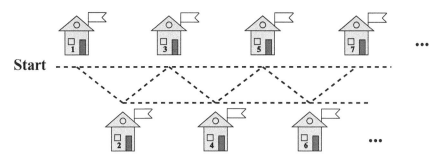

Depending on who gets letters today, he may skip some houses. In how many ways can Rob reach houses #1, #2, #3, #5, and #10?

To help the kids to organize their answers we recommended recording the number of ways to the house on its banner. Once a few kids who missed the diagonal way to house #3 through house #2 were corrected, everybody had the answers 1, 1, 2, 3, and 5 on the banners of houses #1, #2, #3, #4, and #5. At this point the class recognized the Fibonacci sequence, but very few kids were able to explain why the pattern will continue.

It took a few more minutes and tracing all the paths to house #6 for the majority of the class to discover that Rob can get to house #6 only from house #4 or from house #5. While many children could immediately replace various paths to house #4 (or #5) by their count, the rest continued to think of them as a collection of pictures. The latter group would not recognize the importance of the discovery above even if they made it. The following hints helped most of the class to finish the problem:

"What could be the last house Rob passed on his way to house #6?"

"Observe the picture below, where the blue and the red lines denote the ends of the various paths to houses #4 and #5. Draw colored dashed lines to make it clear that the number of paths reaching house #6 is 3 + 5."

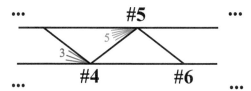

Some children drew the picture on the left, others insisted that the picture on the right with multiple dashed lines is more clear:

Finally, everybody was able to see that the same rule, "the next is the sum of two previous", holds true for all houses. We got the Fibonacci sequence again! There are 55 ways leading to house #10. ■

Fibonacci Sequence in Nature

The answers to many of the preceding problems form one of the most well-known number sequences, the Fibonacci sequence:

$$1, \ 1, \ 2, \ 3, \ 5, \ 8, \ 13, \ \ldots$$

It was first described over two thousand years ago; the earliest records of this sequence go back to the 2nd century BCE in India.

The sequence is called Fibonacci in honor of Leonardo Fibonacci, an Italian mathematician who introduced it to the Western World in 1202 in his book *Liber Abaci*, which means "Book of Calculation".[1]

> **Math Context.** The typical notation for Fibonacci numbers is F_n. The defining recurrence relation is $F_n = F_{n-2} + F_{n-1}$, with starting values $F_1 = 1$, $F_2 = 1$.

---

[1]Handout about Fibonacci's life is on page 167.

Fibonacci numbers appear not only in mathematical contexts — they are often discovered in nature. For instance, the numbers of spirals in many naturally occurring spiral formations turn out to be Fibonacci numbers. They appear in pine cones, like the one shown below with 13 spirals going clockwise and eight spirals going counterclockwise. Observe that 8 and 13 are two consecutive Fibonacci numbers.

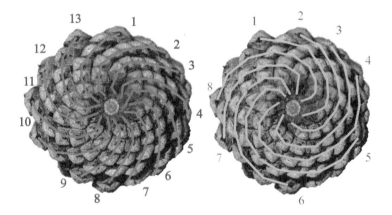

Cacti provide another example. Examining the spirals of the cactus below, one can observe 34 spirals going clockwise and 21 spirals going counterclockwise. Again, 21 and 34 are two consecutive Fibonacci numbers.

In reality when one picks up a random pine cone or a cactus, the spirals may not be as perfect as in the examples above. This happens when the plants get sick or their growth is constrained. It is cheating to count spirals when some are incomplete or to draw fictitious curves. In class we helped the children to confirm that all the red spirals on the left picture are present as whitish curves on the right picture for both cones and cacti. So the kids could see that we had no need to cheat.

Even larger Fibonacci numbers are sometimes found in nature. In sunflowers the number of spirals can be as high as 89 in one direction and 144 in the other.

Although Fibonacci numbers in nature were observed in many ancient cultures long before Fibonacci's time, the general cause of this phenomenon is still debated by modern scientists.

Extension to the Left

Is it possible to extend the Fibonacci sequence to the left? Before we can answer this question one needs to know how to add negative numbers. Many students have not studied negative numbers yet, although most have heard about them. So, we drew the number line:

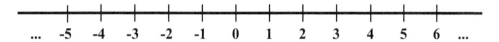

In our experience kids have absolutely no issue with negative numbers appearing on the number line to the left of 0. To expose the kids to the arithmetic with negative numbers we introduced a grasshopper which jumps between numbers in steps of 1. First we placed the grasshopper at 2 on the number line. What should the grasshopper do to model adding 3, 2, 1, or 0 to 2? After getting the answers, we asked the same question about adding -1, or -2, or -3. The class followed the numeric (or pictorial) pattern and concluded: adding a positive number is "moving right", adding 0 is "staying at the same place", and adding a negative number is "moving left". Surprisingly, the children had no problem giving instructions to the grasshopper when it starts at -2.

Problem 3.7. Fibonacci Numbers to the Left of 1, 1. Extend the Fibonacci sequence to the left, so that the numbers still follow the Fibonacci rule: every number is the sum of the two preceding numbers.

A few students fluent with subtraction of negative numbers were able to quickly finish the problem. We helped the rest with the leading questions, starting with, "What should we put instead of '?' in the sequence ?, 1, 1, 2, 3, 5 and why?" Students immediately answered 0. Out of various explanations we selected the one that involved solving $? + 1 = 1$.

"What is '?' in ?, 0, 1, 1, 2, 3, 5 and why?" No one had any doubts that it is 1, and the majority explained it using $? + 0 = 1$.

At this moment many students could proceed by themselves, the rest needed more leading questions.

Many children found "?" in ?, 1, 0, 1, 1, 2, 3, 5 with no difficulty by solving $? + 1 = 0$. Only a couple of students needed a hint, "Where should we place the grasshopper to find '?' in $? + 1 = 0$?"

Finding "?" in the sequence ?, -1, 1, 0, 1, 1, 2, 3, 5 led to a heated discussion. The kids with the correct answer 2 managed to convince the rest of the class using the grasshopper in their arguments.

Soon everybody arrived at the extension ..., 5, −3, 2, −1, 1, 0, 1, 1, 2, 3, 5, ...

"Can you see a pattern?" — "Yes!" The numbers on the left of zero are the same as on the right of zero except for their signs. One can imagine that an enchanted mirror is placed at zero. It preserves the magnitude of the numbers but makes their signs alternate. ∎

At this time we explained to the class that finding "?" on each step of the above problem can be done via subtraction. For example, finding "?" in $? + 1 = 1$ is the same as calculating $1 − 1$. Almost everybody knew it; the kids explained, "Subtraction inverses addition." To test them we asked, "What should the grasshopper do to describe this subtraction?" Again, nobody had doubts that it should start at 1 and jump one step to the left. Several kids pointed out that in addition and subtraction the grasshopper moves in opposite directions.

Now, the class was ready to consider a much more confusing case: subtracting a negative number. When solving $? + (−1) = 1$, we found that $? = 2$. With subtraction, we write it down as $1 − (−1) = 2$. "What should the grasshopper do to model this subtraction?" This led to a short discussion and after a few more examples the class concluded: on the number line, subtracting a positive number "is moving left", subtracting 0 "is staying at the same place", and subtracting a negative number "is moving right". These directions are opposite to those in addition, which makes sense since one can undo addition using subtraction.

> **Math Context.** The Fibonacci sequence may be extended to negative numbers using $F_{n-2} = F_n − F_{n-1}$. So we get:
>
> $$..., \quad −8, \quad 5, \quad −3, \quad 2, \quad −1, \quad 1, \quad 0, \quad 1, \quad 1, \quad 2, \quad 3, \quad 5, \quad 8, \quad ...;$$
>
> moreover $F_{-n} = (−1)^{n+1} F_n$.

Even/Odd Pattern

Analyzing the even/odd pattern of the Fibonacci numbers gave us an opportunity to discuss which numbers are *odd* and which are *even*.

In our classes we observed that the children were taught three different definitions of even numbers:

(1) A number is even if it can be divided into pairs (or can be obtained via "counting by two").
(2) A number is even if it can be split into two equal parts.
(3) A number is even if its last digit is 0, 2, 4, 6, or 8.

In our math circles we work only with the first two definitions. Their equivalence can be easily explained using socks. The number of socks is even if they can be counted by two or paired up. If we now break all pairs putting one sock into the first pile and the other sock into the second pile, we end up splitting the number of socks into two equal parts. This process can be reversed: socks divided into two equal piles can be paired up by taking one sock from the first pile and another sock from the second pile.

For us the third approach is not a definition, but a shortcut to checking whether a number is even. Why does it work? Only a few children could explain without our prompts that any number can be broken into "tens and ones". For example, 435 is 43 tens and 5 ones. Tens can always be broken into two equal parts since $10 = 5 + 5$, so only the last digit matters.

What numbers are odd? Some students tried to formulate a negation of the sentence that defines "even": "Odd numbers cannot be split into two equal parts." Instead, we challenged the class, "Now, when you know what is 'even', you can define 'odd' using fewer words." After a couple of attempts the children arrived at, "Odd means not even."

At this point we needed to establish the "even + even", "even + odd", "odd + even", and "odd + odd" rules. Many students knew these rules but could not explain them.

We like to verify these rules using numbers represented by boxes with socks. We call it the "socks in a box" approach. If the number is even, the socks in the box are paired. If the number is odd, there is one unpaired sock left in the box (this happens if the sock missing from the pair was eaten by a "sock monster"). Combining different boxes gives us the desired rules:

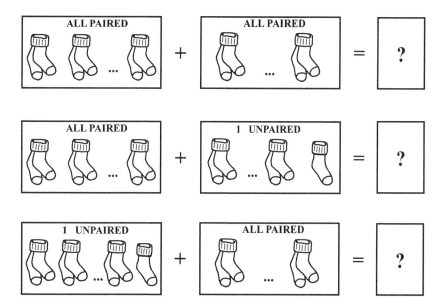

Nobody in our class had any doubt what the results would be in the cases above. Most could also figure out what happens in the last "odd + odd" case. Some students, however, needed to draw an additional picture with two unpaired socks:

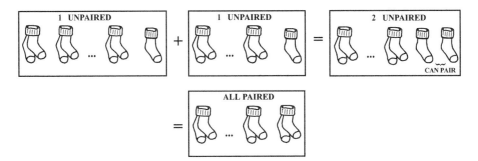

To summarize:

$$\text{EVEN} + \text{EVEN} = \text{EVEN},$$
$$\text{EVEN} + \text{ODD} \ = \text{ODD},$$
$$\text{ODD} + \text{EVEN} = \text{ODD},$$
$$\text{ODD} + \text{ODD} \ = \text{EVEN}.$$

Now we were ready to investigate *parity* (property of numbers to be even or odd) in the Fibonacci sequence:

$$1, \ 1, \ 2, \ 3, \ 5, \ 8, \ 13, \ 21, \ 34, \ 55, \ 89, \ 144, \ \dots$$

The students noticed that numbers in the sequence go in the following order: odd, odd, even, odd, odd, even, ...

Problem 3.8. Even/Odd Pattern. Why does the parity of the Fibonacci numbers repeat in the pattern "odd, odd, even" again and again?

Teacher ▷ This problem is more difficult than typical problems in this book and we guide the children by posing leading questions.

Let's look at the parity of the first few Fibonacci numbers. We use letters "$\mathcal{O}$" and "$\mathcal{E}$" for even and odd to avoid confusion of O and 0:

1	1	2	3	5	8	13
↓	↓	↓	↓	↓	↓	↓
$\mathcal{O}$	$\mathcal{O}$	$\mathcal{E}$	$\mathcal{O}$	$\mathcal{O}$	?	

Number 8 is even and so the "?" is $\mathcal{E}$. Let us cover the framed numbers, 8 and 13, by a piece of paper. Can we still find out whether "?" is even or odd without calculating the sum $3 + 5$? The children immediately shouted "Yes" and provided an explanation: to the left of the "?" we can see $\mathcal{O}\mathcal{O}$ (3 and 5 are both odd). Any $\mathcal{O}\mathcal{O}$ is followed by $\mathcal{E}$, since ODD + ODD = EVEN. Likewise, combinations of $\mathcal{O}$ and $\mathcal{E}$, either $\mathcal{O}\mathcal{E}$ or $\mathcal{E}\mathcal{O}$, will be followed by $\mathcal{O}$.

Now, instead of covering 8 and 13, let us cover all numbers after 1, 1. Then all we know about the second row is that it starts with $\mathcal{O}\mathcal{O}$.

Can the second row be continued as was done before? The children came up with the following picture:

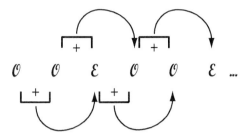

How can we be sure that this pattern continues forever? Many children needed another hint: "When we see $OO\mathcal{E}$ somewhere, what will follow?" Some students found the answer right away; others had to continue the pattern for a little longer. The class concluded: we do not care whether OO starts the Fibonacci sequence or if OO appears anywhere in the sequence, it will always turn into $OO\mathcal{E}OO\mathcal{E}$. So, when we see $OO\mathcal{E}$ it will be followed by $OO\mathcal{E}$ again and again and again! The pattern will repeat forever if it appears once, and we know that it appears at the start.   ■

Divisibility by 3

Teacher ▷ This section is intended for elementary school students who have already studied division.

Let's look at the Fibonacci sequence again, coloring numbers divisible by 3 in red, and numbers not divisible by 3 in blue:

$$1 \ 1 \ 2 \ 3 \ 5 \ 8 \ 13 \ 21 \ 34 \ 55 \ 89 \ 144 \ \ldots$$

As one can see, every fourth number is divisible by 3 (colored in red).

Problem 3.9. Divisibility by 3. Explain why every fourth number in the Fibonacci sequence is divisible by 3.

Several children suggested using a strategy for RED/BLUE numbers similar to the one used for ODD/EVEN numbers in the previous problem.

We decided to check if such a strategy works for the first few Fibonacci numbers:

$$1 + 1 = 2 \qquad \text{BLUE} + \text{BLUE} = \text{BLUE}$$
$$1 + 2 = 3 \qquad \text{BLUE} + \text{BLUE} = \text{RED}$$
$$2 + 3 = 5 \qquad \text{BLUE} + \text{RED} \ = \text{BLUE}$$
$$3 + 5 = 8 \qquad \text{RED} + \text{BLUE} = \text{BLUE}$$

"Can we say something definite about the color of BLUE+BLUE?" — "No!" Looking at the top two rows we see that the result can be different. Apparently, with the divisibility by 2 (EVEN/ODD) we were lucky that "ODD + ODD" is always "EVEN", so we could write the rule for addition:

"ODD + ODD = EVEN". The same approach does not work for divisibility by 3:

$$\text{NON-DIVISIBLE-BY-3} + \text{NON-DIVISIBLE-BY-3}$$

may be of both types, divisible by 3 or not.

That means we have to do more work before we can proceed with the problem. We come back to this problem on page 58 towards the end of this section.

Let us use the "socks in a box" approach again. Consider a family of aliens from Mars who join their socks by threes. "Why by threes?" The children immediately replied, "Obviously because aliens from Mars have three legs!"

Martians keep their socks in boxes and join as many socks in every box as they can into triples. Nevertheless, some socks may remain unjoined — sock monsters eat socks even on Mars! What happens if one combines two such boxes?

Problem 3.10. Triplets of Socks. In a Martian family everybody joins as many socks as possible into triples. Grandpa has a box of socks. Baby has a box of socks too. After combining their socks into one box, all socks may be joined by 3. How could the socks in Grandpa's and Baby's boxes look before they were combined:

- If all Grandpa's socks were joined, what about Baby's socks?
- If Grandpa's box had unjoined socks, how could Baby's box look?

The students realized that there are two separate "Grandpa has unjoined socks" cases: Grandpa has one single sock, or he has two single socks. After that the children quickly came up with the list of three possible situations:

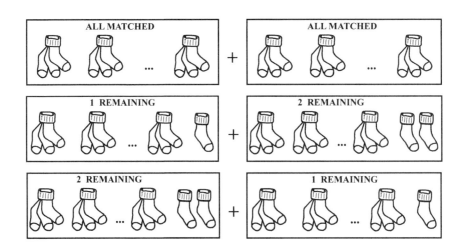

We recorded these results as:

$$0_R + 0_R = 0_R,$$
$$1_R + 2_R = 0_R,$$
$$2_R + 1_R = 0_R.$$

In these equalities 0_R represents a box with zero unjoined socks, 1_R a box with one unjoined sock, and 2_R a box with two unjoined socks. ∎

Problem 3.11. Addition of the Remainders. We already have some entries in the following addition table:

+	0_R	1_R	2_R
0_R	0_R		
1_R			0_R
2_R		0_R	

Fill in the empty cells.

Some of our students filled the empty cells in the table very quickly, while others didn't know how to begin. We suggested imagining or drawing pictures with socks for each cell. A couple of students still struggled, and we helped them to draw a picture for the cell $2_R + 2_R$. In a few minutes everyone filled in the addition table modulo 3:

+	0_R	1_R	2_R
0_R	0_R	1_R	2_R
1_R	1_R	2_R	0_R
2_R	2_R	0_R	1_R

∎

This is an appropriate time to tell the students that the symbols 0_R, 1_R, and 2_R are called *remainders* in math. For example, 11 socks in a box will be joined as $3 + 3 + 3 + 1 + 1$. So, the two unjoined socks "remain" and we say that the remainder is 2 when one divides 11 into groups of 3.

Problem 3.12. Remainders Modulo 3 for Fibonacci Numbers. Replace every Fibonacci number by a box with that many Martian socks. In every box as many socks as possible are joined into triplets. Label every box as 0_R, 1_R, 2_R depending on the number of unjoined socks. Find the pattern in the obtained labels.

Hint: "When labeling a box, do not divide the number of socks by 3; instead, combine the two previous boxes, using the rule for Fibonacci numbers."

Some children still started dividing the Fibonacci numbers by 3. Unfortunately this approach is error-prone and cannot be easily extended to the larger numbers. So we asked the students to switch to the approach suggested by the hint.

With the help of the class we wrote the first few remainders on the board:

- The first two numbers are 1, 1, so we wrote 1_R, 1_R.
- The next number 2 is $1 + 1$; combining two boxes of type 1_R results in a box of type 2_R. Instead of directly finding the box type for number 2, one may just look at the types of two boxes to the left of it!
- The next box type is obtained by combining a box of type 1_R with a box of type 2_R. It is $1_R + 2_R = 0_R$, as shown in the table created in the previous problem.

1	1	2	3	...
1_R	1_R	2_R	0_R	...

A couple of students thought that the sequence would repeat itself in blocks 1_R, 1_R, 2_R, 0_R. We asked these children to write a few more terms of the sequence to confirm their hypothesis.

Pretty soon the group obtained the following:

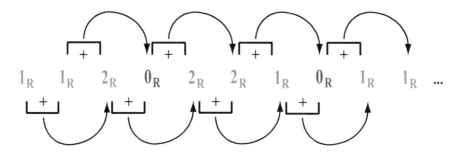

Some children stopped writing the sequence after 1_R, 1_R, 2_R, 0_R, 2_R, 2_R, 1_R, 0_R, 1_R, 1_R saying that 1_R, 1_R at the end means that the sequence is going to repeat itself. Others wrote the sequence further, and after six more additions discovered the repeating pattern.   ∎

Now, let us go back and finish Problem 3.9.

The concluding argument is practically the same as in the even/odd problem, but, as usual, for many children it was hard to articulate why the pattern observed in the previous problem will continue forever. Whenever we see the combination 1_R, 1_R (whether at the start of the Fibonacci sequence or anywhere else) it will be followed by 2_R, 0_R, 2_R, 2_R, 1_R, 0_R. Then it will be followed by 1_R, 1_R again. It means that whenever we see 1_R, 1_R, 2_R, 0_R, 2_R, 2_R, 1_R, 0_R (as a part of the sequence), it is going to be followed by the same part again! Since this part of the sequence appears at the beginning, it will repeat forever.

Inspecting the above sequence, we see that every 4th entry is 0_R, which means that every 4th Fibonacci number is divisible by 3.

This finishes discussion of Problem 3.9.   ∎

Several children asked whether we would see a repeating pattern if we color the Fibonacci numbers divisible by a number different from 2 or 3. We replied, "Yes, but it is a hard problem."

> **Math Context.** The more general statement concerning divisibility of Fibonacci numbers is that if $k|n$, then $F_k|F_n$. Moreover, for every number m, some of F_k are going to be divisible by m. Taking the smallest such k, one may conclude that every kth number is divisible by m.

Sum of the First n Consecutive Fibonacci Numbers

For the sequence of Fibonacci numbers 1, 1, 2, 3, 5, 8, 13, ..., consider the *"running sums"* 1, $1 + 1$, $1 + 1 + 2$, $1 + 1 + 2 + 3$, $1 + 1 + 2 + 3 + 5$, $1 + 1 + 2 + 3 + 5 + 8$, ...

Problem 3.13. Running Sums of the Fibonacci Numbers. Calculate the first few "running sums". Can you find the pattern in the answers? Can you show that the pattern will continue forever?

We began by reminding our students that real mathematicians often make discoveries by first observing a certain pattern, and then finding an explanation for it. This problem asks us to do the same.

We suggested the children use a table for writing the running sums. They quickly filled the two left columns shown below. It took them a couple more minutes to notice that the running sums may be written as a Fibonacci number minus 1 (recorded in the right column):

Running Sum of Fibonacci numbers	Total	Fibonacci number -1
1	**1**	$2 - 1$
$1 + 1$	**2**	$3 - 1$
$1 + 1 + 2$	**4**	$5 - 1$
$1 + 1 + 2 + 3$	**7**	$8 - 1$
$1 + 1 + 2 + 3 + 5$	**12**	$13 - 1$
$1 + 1 + 2 + 3 + 5 + 8$	**20**	$21 - 1$

What is the explanation? Will the pattern continue?

Hint: "Instead of subtracting 1 in the right column, let us add 1 in the left column." Now the "Total" column of the updated table contains Fibonacci numbers. We need to show that if we continue the table, the numbers in the right column will always be Fibonacci numbers.

1 + Sum of Fibonacci numbers	Total
1 + 1	2
1 + 1 + 1	3
1 + 1 + 1 + 2	5
1 + 1 + 1 + 2 + 3	8
1 + 1 + 1 + 2 + 3 + 5	13
1 + 1 + 1 + 2 + 3 + 5 + 8	21

Hint: "Look at the entries in the left columns of the table above. How do they change from row to row?" The kids quickly noticed that they differ only by the last term. Let us modify the table once more. In the left column we put parentheses around the terms that repeat the previous row (in green below). Now all the children realized that the sums in parentheses are already computed; they are "Totals" in the previous row (shown in red). This observation is recorded in the column "Or".

1 + Sum of Fibonacci numbers	Or	Total
1 + 1		2
(1 + 1) + 1	2 + 1	3
(1 + 1 + 1) + 2	3 + 2	5
(1 + 1 + 1 + 2) + 3	5 + 3	8
(1 + 1 + 1 + 2 + 3) + 5	8 + 5	13
(1 + 1 + 1 + 2 + 3 + 5) + 8	13 + 8	21

Thus the green numbers in the middle column (column "Or") are the sums of the numbers in parentheses on the left. At the same time they are copies of the red numbers above on the right (column "Total"). Suppose we already know that a certain red number (for example **13**) is a Fibonacci number. Then the green number in the next row is also a Fibonacci number, and so the sum in the middle column (13 + 8) is a sum of two consecutive Fibonacci numbers. Since the sum of two consecutive Fibonacci numbers is the next Fibonacci number, the next red number (**21**) must also be a Fibonacci number. This pattern will continue forever! ∎

Teacher ▶ This argument lacks an explanation of why the numbers added in the column "Or" are consecutive Fibonacci numbers. Children just stated this fact, but did not notice that they need to prove it. We decided not to focus their attention on this gap.

Math Context. $\sum_{i=0}^{n} F_i = F_{n+2} - 1$. This fact is easily proved by induction.

Fibonacci Rectangles and Fibonacci Spiral

Problem 3.14. A Mathematical Fairy Tale.

- In the middle of a beautiful forest an Ant builds a house. The house has one square room (the small grey square in the picture below).
- A Ladybug loves the place and wants to live there too; so she extends the house by attaching another square room on the right (the small square to the right of the first one).
- A Snail comes, loves the place, and attaches another square room for herself. Since the Snail is larger, she attaches the room on the bottom.
- This process is repeated by the Mouse, who attaches a square room on the left.
- The house extension is continued by a Rabbit, a Fox, a Lion, and so on.

Extensions are attached in the clockwise direction shown by the arrows: first →; then ↓; then ←; and so on.

(a) Show that if we continue adding larger and larger rooms for the creatures, the sides of the rooms will always be Fibonacci numbers.

(b) Show that after each addition the sides of the house will also form a Fibonacci sequence.

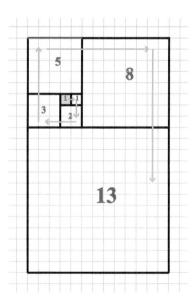

Before starting this problem we asked the children a couple of leading questions.

"What is the shape of the house after each addition?" It's a rectangle. The first house, the Ant's, is a square but squares are also rectangles.

At this moment we discussed what a rectangle is and listed its properties on the board. One of these properties, the equality of opposite sides, is essential for the solution.

"Can you draw the next room, which belongs to a Hippo?" Almost everyone in the class drew the next square with side 21 without any problem. All the students were sure that the sides of the rectangles form the Fibonacci sequence, but most could not explain why.

Let us look at the side of the largest square room in the picture above, 13. The top side is the sum of the sides of the three smaller squares: $3 + 2 + 8$. However, Fibonacci numbers are formed by a different rule: they are the sum of two (not three) previous numbers! To follow the Fibonacci sequence the sides of the squares should be equal to the sum of the sides of the two previous squares, $13 = 5 + 8$. The 8×8 square is next to the 13×13 square, but the 5×5 square is not, and so several children needed a hint: "On the picture mark the part which illustrates the addition of $5+8$." After marking this on the top side of the picture, almost everybody noticed that the segments of length 3, 2, and 8, and the segments 5 and 8 form two opposite sides of the 8×13 rectangle (the house after the Fox's addition). Hence they have the same length!

On every step of the house expansion the longer side of the rectangle is the sum of the sides of the two largest rooms. This means that every new square has a side equal to the sum of the sides of the two previous squares. Hence, the sides of the squares form a Fibonacci sequence.

It wasn't very hard for the students to notice that the smaller side of the rectangle is equal to the side of the last added square, and the larger side to the side of the next square-to-add. Since the sides of the squares form the Fibonacci sequence, the sides of the rectangles also form a Fibonacci sequence.   ■

These rectangles (the houses) are called *Fibonacci rectangles*.

Problem 3.15. Running Sums of Squares of Fibonacci Numbers.
Observe:

$$1^2 + 1^2 = 1 \times 2,$$
$$1^2 + 1^2 + 2^2 = 2 \times 3,$$
$$1^2 + 1^2 + 2^2 + 3^2 = 3 \times 5,$$
$$1^2 + 1^2 + 2^2 + 3^2 + 5^2 = 5 \times 8.$$

Will the pattern continue? Why?
Hint: "Remember the Fibonacci rectangles."

The majority of the class did not compute the sum on the left or the product on the right. Instead they identified the summands on the left and the factors on the right with the house from the Mathematical Fairy Tail. At each step of the house extension the area of the whole house is the sum of the areas of the Fibonacci squares (individual rooms). This verifies the equality, and the pattern will continue forever! ∎

We finished the discussion of the Fibonacci rectangles with a couple of interesting curves. If we draw a quarter of a circle in each square, we get a spiral-like blue curve:

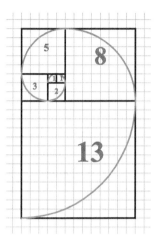

If we had a magnifying glass we would see the "ugly" junctions at the ends of the quarter-circles. There is a way to change the quarter-circles into a better-matching curve called the *Fibonacci log-spiral*. This log-spiral looks "smoother" but with the help of a magnifying glass one could see tiny discrepancies: it does not go exactly through the corners of the squares. The smaller the square, the larger the discrepancy. Still, it is really amazing how good the match is for the larger squares.

Teacher ▶ The log-spiral is much "smoother", but nevertheless does not go exactly through the corners of the squares. Our children are too young to understand what a Fibonacci logarithmic spiral is. The Fibonacci sequence matches a geometric progression with ratio φ well, but it doesn't match it exactly.

The log-spiral is often seen in nature; for example, snail shells often fit the Fibonacci log-spiral. However, a lot of such coincidences are just wishful thinking. For example, some people claim that the curves of a human ear match the Fibonacci log-spiral.

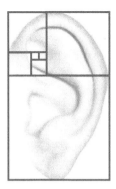

Can you find where the flaws are in this match? The children greatly
enjoyed finding them, although some needed our help: "Look at the corners
of the squares. On which curve of the ear are they positioned?" The corners
of the squares lay on different spirals.

Honeybees' Ancestral Tree

Leonardo Fibonacci obtained his sequence modeling the procreation of rabbits. The following problem is about honeybees' ancestry tree. It is also
biological, but more realistic and much easier to formulate.

Ancestry trees, unlike family trees, show only direct ancestors: parents,
grandparents, great-grandparents, and so on, but they do not show siblings.
In an ancestry tree the parents can be drawn above or below their child. We
will draw them above.

Female honeybees have two parents, a male and a female, whereas male
honeybees (drones) have just one parent, a female:

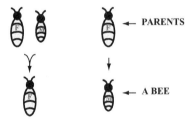

Problem 3.16. Small Ancestry Tree. Draw an ancestry tree of a drone.
Go back to the 4th generation.

The children promptly produced the following picture:

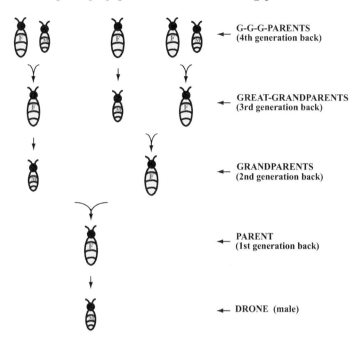

Problem 3.17. Ancestors of Honeybees. How many ancestors does a drone have in generations 5, 6, and 10?

Teacher This problem is complicated, so we discuss it at the end of the chapter, guiding students with a lot of hints.

First, the class counted bees in each generation in the above picture and was amazed to discover a familiar sequence: 1, 1, 2, 3, 5. The students understood that they need to explain that the next number in the sequence is the sum of the previous two, but had no clue why. Hint: "Count males and females in each generation separately and record the results in a table." The results are:

Generation (back)	0	1	2	3	4	5	6	7
Number of male ancestors	1	0	1	1	2			
Number of female ancestors	0	1	1	2	3			
Total number of ancestors	1	1	2	3	5			

"Can you draw a bigger ancestry tree and fill in the remaining columns of the table?" The students like drawing the big ancestry trees and had no problem with getting the answers, shown in the next table. They observed that the number of male ancestors, female ancestors, and the total number of ancestors form Fibonacci sequences. However, the sequence for the male ancestors begins with 1, 0, 1; for the female ancestors it begins with 0, 1, 1; and for the total amount of ancestors it begins with 1, 1, 2. So, there are shifts in the Fibonacci sequence in the table.

Generation (back)	0	1	2	3	4	5	6	7
Male	1	0	1	1	2	3	5	8
Female	0	1	1	2	3	5	8	13
Total	1	1	2	3	5	8	13	21

Why do all the rows in the table above form Fibonacci sequences?

Hint: "Look at the repeating numbers in the diagonals of the table and try to explain the equality. For example, why is the number of female bees in the 5th generation back equal to the total of bees in the 4th generation back?" Some of the students came up with the explanations similar to: "It's an ancestry tree, so each female has a child, and the number of children is displayed on the left in the 'Total' row."

Now a couple of students anticipated our next question and voiced it on their own, "Why is the number of males in the 6th generation back equal to the number of females in the 5th generation back?" While this question was harder, the children were in the right mindset, "Every male in the ancestry tree has one daughter, and the daughters are displayed on the left." There is one exception to this claim, the first drone child, but we did not mention it in class.

Now we have an explanation of the diagonal repetitions in the table. Is it possible to use them to find "?" in the table below?

Male	1	0	1	1	...				
Female	0	1	1	2	...				
Total	1	1	2	3	...	34	55	?	

The students knew that it should be "89" but it was just a guess, based on continuing the Fibonacci sequence. We required an explanation and gave a hint: "Think diagonally!" The children filled the table, using the already explained diagonal patterns:

Male	1	0	1	1	...			34	55
Female	0	1	1	2	...		34	55	
Total	1	1	2	3	...	34	55	?	

Look at the column with red numbers 34, 55, and "?":

- The red 34 in the top row is the count of males; in the bottom row black 34 stands for the total number of bees 2 generations prior to "?".

- The red 55 in the second row is the count of females; in the bottom row black 55 stands for the total number of bees 1 generation prior to "?".

The total number of bees in a certain generation is the sum of females and males in that generation. So, finding the total we sum up numbers circled in red; but instead we can sum up numbers circled in green:

Therefore, we end up with the Fibonacci sequence, where any number starting with the third is the sum of two previous numbers. Hence, the drone has eight ancestors in the 5th generation back, 13 ancestors in the 6th generation back, and 89 in the 10th generation back. ■

Chapter 4

Pascal's Triangle

We usually spend almost the entire term discussing the properties of Pascal's triangle. When later we draw an equilateral or even an isosceles triangle on the board and ask the children what triangle it is, most of them reply without any hesitation: "It is Pascal's triangle!"

Paths in Mouseville

Problem 4.1. Paths in Mouseville. In Mouseville (known in other places as Nowhere York) a red star marks Mice Elementary School. The houses of the mice Anny, Bobby, Conny, Danny, Eddy, Freddy, and Ginny are marked by the letters A through G. The mice always take the shortest routes from school to their homes. Who has the largest number of different paths home? How many?

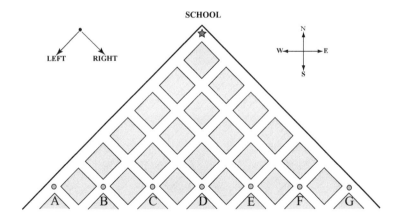

Before solving the problem we asked the students to give examples of Bobby's and Danny's possible paths home. The class suggested that Bobby goes ✓ 4 times, then ↘, then again ✓ (see the red dashed line below), and that Danny goes ✓ first, then ↘, then another ↘, then ✓, ↘, ✓ (see the

solid blue path below). There are many other possible routes for both of
them.

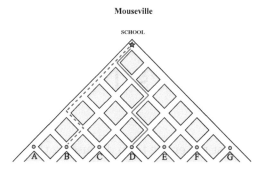

To solve the problem we need to find exactly how many paths lead to
each house. Many students immediately observed that there is only one
path leading to Anny's house: ✓ ✓ ✓ ✓ ✓ ✓. At the same time several
children noticed that the map is symmetric, and so there should be the same
number of paths to houses A and G, to houses B and F, and to houses C
and E.

"What about the paths to Bobby's house?" The children wanted to
draw all of his routes. So, we distributed the handouts with the map of
Mouseville and reviewed why mice never go up. This follows from counting
only the shortest paths, as was previously discussed in Problem 2.7, Chapter
2, "Combinatorics". The children drew all six possible paths:

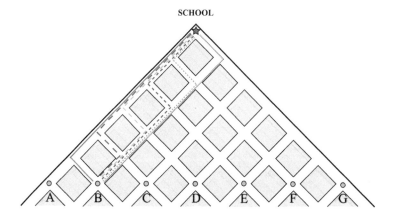

Teacher Using colored pencils helps to ensure no paths are missed and none are repeated
twice.

Then the children attempted to draw Conny's routes but soon realized
that the task is formidable. Instead, the kids decided to list all of her routes.
Since the arrows the kids draw are often sloppy and hard to distinguish, we
proposed to use the letter L to denote going left, and the letter R to denote

going right at any intersection. In this notation one of the paths to C is LRLLRL. Only a couple of the kids remembered that they worked with similar strings in Problem 2.7, Chapter 2, "Combinatorics".

How would all paths to C look in this notation? The children wrote down a few paths and discovered that all of them consist of six letters and contain two letter Rs. Why? To help the kids to verbalize the explanation we provided the following picture:

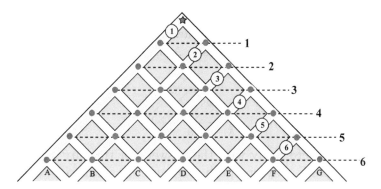

The children explained that at each intersection (marked by red dots in the picture above) Conny chooses to go either to the left or to the right. In both cases, she goes one level down and in total she descends six levels (levels are marked by dashed lines). Every time Conny goes right (the letter R), she ends up on a yellow diagonal with a larger number. Going left (the letter L), she stays on the same diagonal. Going home, Conny starts on the first diagonal and will end on the third diagonal, which means she must make exactly two right steps. Thus, each path to house C is an arrangement of two Rs and four Ls.

Only some of the students remembered how to list all possible paths systematically; the rest required our help. Since this topic was discussed in detail in Chapter 2, "Combinatorics", we will skip this part here. Eventually the children came up with the list:

RRLLLL RLRLLL RLLRLL RLLLRL RLLLLR
LRRLLL LRLRLL LRLLRL LRLLLR
LLRRLL LLRLRL LLRLLR
LLLRRL LLLRLR
LLLLRR

Hence, the total number of paths to C is $15 = 5 + 4 + 3 + 2 + 1$. Many students recognized that this is a triangular number. Later we will see that this is not a coincidence but a part of a pattern.

A couple of children pointed out that the number of paths to B, 6, is also a triangular number. However, this is a coincidence: if the city on the map were smaller or larger (had fewer or more levels), the number of paths to B may not be a triangular number, as we will soon discover.

Now we know how many paths lead to every house but D. The kids were not thrilled by the prospect of listing all possible paths to D; even for C it was a long and tedious job. "Can we be smart and find a better method that works for D and would work even for larger cities?"

Working on complicated problems in the preceding chapters, we found that considering a simplified version of a problem often helps to find a solution. Recall, for instance, how we figured out parking problems in Chapter 3, "Fibonacci Numbers". "What 'smaller and simpler' problem should we consider now?" The children immediately suggested computing the number of paths for a smaller map with fewer houses and mice. The map we considered first had only three houses, A, B, and C:

The children were ready with the answers for this city map faster than we drew it. There is only one path to A and one path to C, and there are two paths to B: LR and RL.

Next, the children decided to look at the map with four houses. "Do we need to draw a new map for each smaller problem? Or can we somehow use the map of Mouseville?" Pretty quickly many students proposed to cover the bottom of the original map instead of drawing a new one. They pointed out that counting the number of paths leading to the houses on a smaller map is the same as counting the number of paths leading to the intersections in the original map.

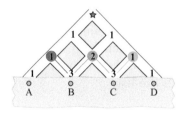

What is the number of paths to each of the houses A, B, C, and D? There is only one path to A and to D. A number of students noticed that in order to get to B a mouse needs to go either through the intersection marked by a red dot and turn right or through the intersection marked by the orange dot and turn left. There are no other ways of getting to B. This means that the number of paths leading to B is the number of paths leading to the red dot plus the number of paths leading to the orange dot: $1 + 2 = 3$. This is the same idea as in the "Postman Rob" problem (Problem 3.6, Chapter 3, "Fibonacci Numbers").

In a few minutes the whole class was sure that the same approach would work for any intersection in Mouseville that is not on the left or right border of the map: a mouse can come to it only from one of the two intersections above. Hence, the number of paths leading to such intersection is the sum of the numbers of paths leading to the two intersections above it.

Now we are ready to get back to the question: "How can we compute the number of paths to Danny's house in the original map?" We gave the students the handout with the map of Mouseville to write down the number of paths to each intersection. They immediately put 1s on the left and right borders. They proceeded to compute the rest of the numbers level by level using the rule stated above and obtained:

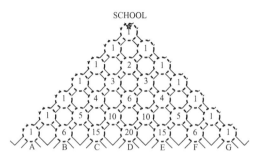

The entries in the last row are the numbers of paths leading to the mice's houses. In particular, there are 20 ways leading to Danny's house; this is the largest number of paths compared to the number of paths leading to any other house. ■

As the students computed the number of paths to each intersection in Mouseville and wrote these numbers in the handout, some of them noticed that the map of Nowhere York (Problem 2.7, Chapter 2, "Combinatorics") and the map of Mouseville are very similar. If Mouseville's map is rotated and some parts of it are covered, it looks like the map of Nowhere York. Red circles show the possible locations of Andy's home in Nowhere York.

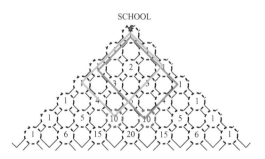

Keeping only the numbers on the map of Mouseville we get a beautiful triangle. It is called *Pascal's triangle* after French mathematician Blaise Pascal,[1] although other mathematicians studied it centuries before him in India, Persia, China, Germany, and Italy.

---

[1] The handout with Pascal's biography is on page 168.

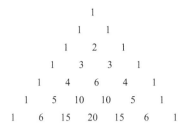

This triangle consists of "1"s on the left and right sides. All other numbers inside the triangle are defined by the Pascal's triangle rule: each number is a sum of two numbers above it.

Teacher Later in the chapter we will extend Pascal's triangle to the whole plane. Until then, when we refer to the Pascal's triangle rule, it is implied that it works for the numbers inside the triangle and that the left and right edges consist of ones.

To confirm that everybody understood the Pascal's triangle rule we invited the students to take turns coming up to the board and writing more rows of Pascal's triangle. The children joked that they will spend years doing it — Pascal's triangle can be continued forever.

Hockey Stick Pattern

Let us look at diagonals in Pascal's triangle starting with 1. For example, consider the numbers highlighted in yellow below: $1, 6, 21, 56, 126, \ldots$. Now compute the running sums: $1 + 6 = 7$, $1 + 6 + 21 = 28$, $1 + 6 + 21 + 56 = 84$, $1 + 6 + 21 + 56 + 126 = 210$, and so on. The children noticed right away that each running sum is a number in Pascal's triangle located immediately below and to the right of the last summand. For instance, 210 is below 126 to the right.

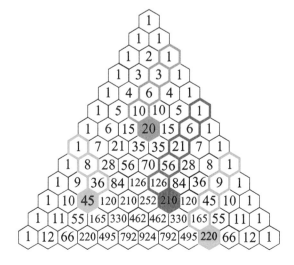

Does this pattern hold for the running sums that start with 1 on other diagonals? The students eagerly checked a few sums and confirmed, "Yes, it does, but the sum is below the last summand to the right for diagonals going down left, and below to the left for diagonals going down right." This pattern is called a *"Hockey Stick pattern"*; the numbers that are being added (summands) form a shaft and the sum is a blade.

Problem 4.2. Hockey Stick. Explain the Hockey Stick pattern. Hint: "Use the Pascal's triangle rule."

Since this problem contains a general statement, the students didn't know how to begin. Hint: "Explain why the pattern works for a certain stick, for example, for the stick outlined in red **1+6+21+56+126**." The children explained that the addition of numbers **1 + 6** on the shaft can be replaced by the addition of **6 + 1**, both located in the seventh row. Since **6** and 1 are next to each other in the same row, their sum is number 7 below by the Pascal's triangle rule. Since 7 and the shaft's **21** are adjacent numbers in the same row, their sum is number 28 below (again the Pascal's triangle rule). Similarly, 28 and the shaft's **56** are next to each other in the same row. Their sum is the number below, 84. Finally, 84 and the shaft's **126** are also two adjacent numbers in the same row. Their sum is the number **210** below.

The students argued that the same process would work for any hockey stick starting with 1: the shaft might be shorter or longer but the pattern holds. We did not insist on the general proof.   ∎

Diagonals in Pascal's Triangle

Teacher ► In this section we review some of the material from Chapter 1, "Numbers as Geometric Shapes", but tie it to Pascal's triangle. In our experience many children forget how to solve those problems and it is worth repeating some of them.

When teaching young children we number rows and diagonals of Pascal's triangle starting with one instead of the usual zero because the children are used to counting from one and get confused by the zeroth row or diagonal.

Problem 4.3. Diagonals in Pascal's Triangle. What patterns do you observe in the diagonals of Pascal's triangle? Explain them.

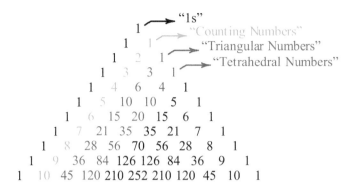

The children immediately pointed out that the first diagonal (shown in black) is all 1s because there is only one path to house A in a Mouseville of any size.

Everybody noticed that the second diagonal (shown in green) contains consecutive numbers. Many kids explained that each number on this diagonal (except 1) is the sum of a green number above it and 1 according to Pascal's triangle rule. Other students recalled the Hockey Stick problem: each green number is a sum of 1s from the first diagonal. So moving down from row to row one gets consecutive numbers.

The pattern in the third diagonal (shown in red) is not obvious but some students still recognized consecutive triangular numbers. Once someone named the pattern, many children were able to explain it. The majority of the students stated that any triangular number is a sum of consecutive numbers starting with 1, and that is exactly what we get from the hockey sticks with shafts on the 2nd diagonal. Only a couple of kids used the Pascal's triangle rule in their explanation.

The children had to think about the fourth blue diagonal for a couple of minutes before some of them figured out that it contains tetrahedral numbers. Almost everyone who could explain this observation used the Hockey Stick pattern. Every blue number is the sum of several consecutive triangular numbers in the red diagonal starting with 1. The children suggested making the corresponding triangles out of balls and arranging them to make a tetrahedral (or triangular) pyramid as was discussed in Problem 1.24, Chapter 1, "Numbers as Geometric Shapes".

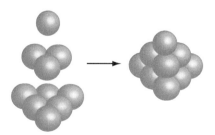

Before stating the next problem we asked the class, "Why is the sum of two consecutive numbers in the red diagonal always a square?" Many children remembered Problem 1.15, "Sum of Two Consecutive Triangular Numbers", and answered, "The sum of two consecutive triangular numbers is always a square."

Problem 4.4. Sums of Consecutive Squares. Find a way to quickly add consecutive squares starting with 1^2 using Pascal's triangle.

Teacher ▶ Before solving this problem we reviewed Problems 1.28, "Square Pyramid" and 1.29, "Splitting a Square Pyramid".

Hint: "First consider the sum $1^2 + 2^2 + 3^2 + 4^2$." The students easily noticed that the sum $1^2 + 2^2 + 3^2 + 4^2$ represents the number of balls in the square pyramid of height four. This pyramid can be split into two tetrahedral pyramids of height four and three, and the number of balls in each of them can be found in Pascal's triangle. The kids were thrilled to discover that the sum $1^2 + 2^2 + 3^2 + 4^2$ can be computed by adding only two numbers from Pascal's triangle: $1^2 + 2^2 + 3^2 + 4^2 = 20 + 10$. They argued that this method should work for longer sums. For example, $1^2 + 2^2 + 3^2 + 4^2 + 5^2 + 6^2 + 7^2 = 140 = 84 + 56$, the sum of the seventh and sixth numbers on the blue diagonal of Pascal's triangle. ∎

Rows in Pascal's Triangle

Problem 4.5. Sum of Numbers in a Row. Calculate the sums of numbers in every row for the first few rows of Pascal's triangle. Find the pattern and explain it.

The students quickly calculated sums for each of the first four rows of Pascal's triangle, and easily deduced the pattern: the totals double from row to row. The next few sums were calculated by doubling.

					1						1
				1		1					2
			1		2		1				4
		1		3		3		1			8
	1		4		6		4		1		16
1		5		10		10		5		1	32
1	6	15		20		15		6		1	64

"Are you sure that the pattern will continue?" The majority of the children required our help to explain the pattern. Hint: "Look at the sum of the numbers in the 4th row: $1 + 3 + 3 + 1 = 8$. Show that the sum of the numbers in the next row is twice larger without directly calculating the sum but using the Pascal's triangle rule."

Only a few children managed to explain it without further hints: "Color four numbers in the fourth row: **1, 3, 3,** 1. Write the numbers in the fifth row as sums preserving colors." The students wrote the bottom row shown below without any difficulties.

$$
\begin{array}{cccccccc}
& \mathbf{1} & & \mathbf{3} & & \mathbf{3} & & 1 \\
\mathbf{1} & & \mathbf{1}+\mathbf{3} & & \mathbf{3}+\mathbf{3} & & \mathbf{3}+1 & & 1
\end{array}
$$

The children observed that every number in the top row appears in the bottom row exactly two times. Hence, the sum of numbers in the fifth row is twice bigger than the sum of numbers in the fourth row.

To convince everybody that the same argument would work for any row, we replaced the numbers with toys of different shapes (see the top row in the picture below). "What should one draw in the row below if one follows the rules of Pascal's triangle?"

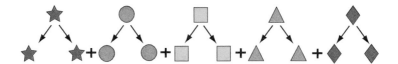

The children promptly drew the second row (see the picture above). "Why does the total price of the toys in the bottom row equal twice the price of the toys in the top row?" We received a perfect explanation: "Each toy from the top row appears exactly twice in the bottom row, and so the total price of the toys in the bottom row is twice the total for the top row. The particular prices of the toys do not matter."

Finally, the children could clearly see that no matter what numbers and how many of them are there in any row of Pascal's triangle, the sum of all numbers in the next row would be twice bigger.   ∎

We asked the class to compute the sum of all numbers in the 11th row of Pascal's triangle. Since the sum doubles from row to row and for the first row it is 1, the sum is $2 \times 2 \times 2 \times 2 \times 2 \times 2 \times 2 \times 2 \times 2 \times 2 \times 1 = 2^{10} = 1024$. We will use this approximation to estimate the sums of numbers in some other rows of Pascal's triangle.

Problem 4.6. Approximate the Sum of Numbers in a Row. What is the approximate sum of numbers in the 21st row of Pascal's triangle? In the 31st row? In the 41st row?

In a couple of minutes many children claimed they know the answer to the first question. To our surprise, their opinions varied from 10,000 to 100,000, to 1,000,000. What is the right answer?

Hint: "Remember that doubling 1 ten times is approximately 1000." Soon several students explained that to get the sum of numbers in the 21st row, the sum of numbers in the 11th row should be doubled 10 times. Since doubling 10 times is approximately the same as multiplying by 1,000, the approximate result is $1,000 \times 1,000 = 1,000,000$, a million.

Others intended to get the total for the 21st row by doubling 1 twenty times but got stuck and needed an additional hint: "How can we split doubling 20 times?" Together with the class we drew the following diagram and obtained the same result: $1,000 \times 1,000 = 1,000,000$.

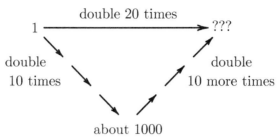

To find the sum of numbers in the 31st row of Pascal's triangle, some children doubled 10 times the result obtained for the 21st row. This is approximately $1,000 \times 1,000,000 = 1,000,000,000$, a billion. Other kids used the second method described above: they split doubling 1 thirty times into doubling 20 times followed by doubling 10 times, and received the same answer.

Finally, the class obtained the sum of numbers in the 41st row of Pascal's triangle by doubling 10 times the total for the 31st row. It is approximately $1,000 \times 1,000,000,000 = 1,000,000,000,000$, a trillion. ∎

Teacher ▶ Warmup Problems 6.11, 6.12 should be given a couple of weeks prior to the next problem.

Problem 4.7. Sum of Numbers. Find the sum of numbers in the first 10 rows of Pascal's triangle.

Several students immediately started to add $1 + 2 + 4 + 8 + 16 + 32 + 64 + 128 + 256 + 512$, which took them a long time.

Others remembered the warmup Problems 6.11 and 6.12, and quickly found the correct answer:
$1 + 2 + 4 + 8 + 16 + 32 + 64 + 128 + 256 + 512 = 2 \times 512 - 1 = 1024 - 1 = 1023$. ∎

Extending Pascal's Triangle

We asked the children, "Does every number in Pascal's triangle equal the sum of two numbers above it?" The children replied, "No, it is not true for the 1s on the sides and on the top of the triangle."

Problem 4.8. Extending Pascal's Triangle. Extend Pascal's triangle so that any number is a sum of two numbers above it.

First, consider the 1s on the sides, but not on the top, of Pascal's triangle. There is only one number above each of them. To get these 1s to follow the

Pascal's triangle rule we need to add numbers to the left and to the right of the triangle. Some children knew how to do it right away, while others needed a hint: "What number should be added to 1 to get 1?" The kids shouted, "Of course, 0!" and added green 0s on both sides of the 1s as shown below. These 0s should follow Pascal's triangle rule too. So, the lilac 0s were added to the picture. Finally, the kids realized that there are infinitely many 0s on both sides of the 1s.

···	0	0	0	0	0	0	1	0	0	0	0	0	0		···
···	0	0	0	0	0	0	1	1	0	0	0	0	0	0	···
···	0	0	0	0	0	1	2	1	0	0	0	0	0		···
···	0	0	0	0	0	1	3	3	1	0	0	0	0	0	···
···	0	0	0	0	1	4	6	4	1	0	0	0	0		···
···	0	0	0	0	1	5	10	10	5	1	0	0	0	0	···
···	0	0	0	1	6	15	20	15	6	1	0	0	0		···
···	0	0	0	1	7	21	35	35	21	7	1	0	0	0	···
···	0	0	1	8	28	56	70	56	28	8	1	0	0		···

The Pascal's triangle rule still breaks in the top row. Can we fix it? The children suggested adding a row above. They started putting 0s from left to right as shown below until they realized that "$?_1$" cannot be 0; it should be 1.

···	0	0	0	0	0	0	0	$?_1$	$?_2$	$?_3$	$?_4$	$?_5$	$?_6$	$?_7$ ···
···	0	0	0	0	0	0	1	0	0	0	0	0	0	···
···	0	0	0	0	0	1	1	0	0	0	0	0	0	···
···	0	0	0	0	0	1	2	1	0	0	0	0	0	···
···	0	0	0	0	0	1	3	3	1	0	0	0	0	···
···	0	0	0	0	1	4	6	4	1	0	0	0	0	···
···	0	0	0	0	1	5	10	10	5	1	0	0	0	···

After reviewing negative numbers, which were discussed in Chapter 3, "Fibonacci Numbers", most kids had no difficulties replacing other "?"s with a row of alternating positive and negative ones: $-1, 1, -1, 1, -1, 1, -1, \ldots$.

Now the Pascal's triangle rule does not work for the newly created row. The children suggested to add another row above, and another row after that, and yet another row after that. They were sure that the extended Pascal's triangle will cover the entire plane and pretty soon came up with quite a few more rows of this extension:

```
                        0  0  0  0  0  0  0  0  0  0 1
                      0  0  0  0  0  0  0  0  0  0 1 –8
                    0  0  0  0  0  0  0  0  0  0 1 –7 28
                  0  0  0  0  0  0  0  0  0  0 1 –6 21 –56
                0  0  0  0  0  0  0  0  0  0 1 -5 15 –35 70
              0  0  0  0  0  0  0  0  0  0 1 –4 10 -20 35 –56
            0  0  0  0  0  0  0  0  0  0 1 –3 6 –10 15 –21 28
          0  0  0  0  0  0  0  0  0  0 1 –2 3 –4 5 –6 7 –8
        0  0  0  0  0  0  0  0  0  0 1 –1 1 –1 1 –1 1 -1 1
      0  0  0  0  0  0  0  0  0 1 0 0 0 0 0 0 0 0
        0  0  0  0  0  0  0  0 1 1 0 0 0 0 0 0 0
          0  0  0  0  0  0  0 1 2 1 0 0 0 0 0 0
            0  0  0  0  0  0 1 3 3 1 0 0 0 0 0
              0  0  0  0 1 4 6 4 1 0 0 0 0
                0  0  0 1 5 10 10 5 1 0 0 0
                  0  0 1 6 15 20 15 6 1 0 0
                    0 1 7 21 35 35 21 7 1 0
                      1 8 28 56 70 56 28 8 1
```

Once this result appeared on the board, the students became impatient and yelled, "We see patterns!" Several kids noticed that if the signs of the numbers in the red triangle are ignored, the red triangle looks like the rotated blue one. Other observations made by the children were variations of this one. For example, several students focused their attention on the red rows of the extended triangle (horizontal lines). Most of the kids ignored the signs and stated that the numbers in the rows are the same as in the diagonals of the original blue triangle. A couple of children pointed out that the signs in the red rows are alternating: $+, -, +, -, \ldots$. Other students looked at the red diagonals going down left. Ignoring signs, these diagonals look like flipped up or reflected diagonals of the original blue triangle. The signs of those diagonals alternate. Yet another group of students pointed out that the red diagonals going down right are similar to the rows of the original blue triangle but the numbers have alternating signs. ■

"Is it the only way to extend Pascal's triangle to the whole plane?" A number of students quickly noticed that we could have started the extension up from right to left (instead of from left to right) getting a mirror image of the above result. Actually, there are many other ways to extend Pascal's triangle to the whole plane. We would like to explore a way that preserves the mirror symmetry of Pascal's triangle. To get a unique answer, we need to put additional constraints on some of the entries.

Teacher ▶ To solve the next problem the children should be able to work with simplest fractions: halves.

Problem 4.9. Extending Pascal's Triangle Symmetrically. Starting with Pascal's triangle extended to the sides, extend it up following these rules:

- The Pascal's triangle rule: Every number is equal to the sum of two numbers above it.

- The Symmetry Rule: In every row, the numbers at equal distances from the symmetry line are equal to each other.
- The Uniqueness Rule: The extension must have zeros on the symmetry line.

We gave the children a handout with Pascal's triangle extended to the sides and with 0s on the symmetry line above 1 in the top row of the regular Pascal's triangle. We asked, "What numbers should replace the two '?'s in the first row up?"

```
                              ?   ?
··· 0  0  0  0  0  0  0 1  0  0  0  0  0  0 ···
··· 0  0  0  0  0  0  0 1  1  0  0  0  0  0  0···
···  0  0  0  0  0  0 1  2  1  0  0  0  0  0 ···
··· 0  0  0  0  0  0 1  3  3  1  0  0  0  0  0···
···  0  0  0  0  0 1  4  6  4  1  0  0  0  0 ···
··· 0  0  0  0 1  5 10 10  5  1  0  0  0  0 ···
```

According to the symmetry rule, these numbers split one into two equal parts. The kids easily determined that each "?" should be replaced by "$\frac{1}{2}$" since $\frac{1}{2} + \frac{1}{2} = 1$. Then, they wrote down other numbers in that row using the Pascal's triangle rule. All numbers turned out to be either $\frac{1}{2}$ or $-\frac{1}{2}$. Filling the rest of the numbers in the handout, the children occasionally made arithmetical errors, but enjoyed the exercise. Their result is shown below with all entries written as fractions with denominator 2 to better display the patterns. The children were excited when they noticed that the numerators are the same as the numbers in the red triangle calculated in the previous problem. Even the signs are the same.

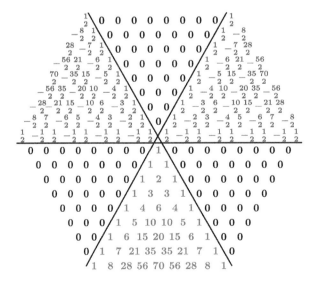

Fibonacci Numbers in Pascal's Triangle

There is another familiar pattern hiding in Pascal's triangle. To see it better we used a bulldozer to realign the rows:

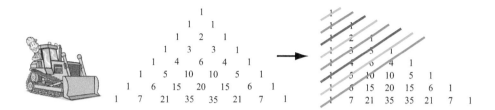

Now let us look at the diagonals in the realigned triangle (see the right picture above).

Problem 4.10. Fibonacci Numbers in Pascal's Triangle. Calculate the sum of numbers for each colored diagonal in the right picture above. Find and explain the pattern.

The children calculated the sums of the numbers on every diagonal, 1, 1, 2, 3, 5, 8, 13, and 21, and immediately recognized the Fibonacci sequence. In that sequence every number starting with the third is a sum of two previous numbers.

Explaining why the pattern should continue turned out to be challenging. Hint: "Formulate the Pascal's triangle rule for the realigned Pascal's triangle." Comparing numbers in the two triangles shown below, the children noticed that for the right picture the Pascal's triangle rule should be modified: each number is a sum of two numbers, one above it, and one above and to the left. Here we assume that there are invisible zeros on both sides of the triangles. Essentially, bulldozing makes every $\triangledown$-triangle of numbers into a $\triangledown$-triangle.

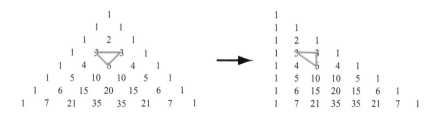

Once the children visualized the Pascal's triangle rule, some solved the problem on their own. We helped the rest to come up with the following picture that makes it easier to explain the recursive relation:

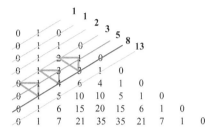

The students observed that each number on the red diagonal is a sum of two numbers on the corners of the corresponding orange triangle. One of these numbers belongs to the green diagonal and the other to the blue diagonal. Writing it down in color the children got:

$$
\begin{array}{rcl}
1 &=& 1 + 0 \\
+ \quad 4 &=& 3 + 1 \\
\hline
3 &=& 1 + 2 \\
\hline
8 &=& 5 + 3
\end{array}
$$

So, the total of all the numbers on the red diagonal is the total of all the numbers on the green diagonal plus the total of all the numbers on the blue diagonal. In other words, the total for the red diagonal is the sum of totals for the two previous diagonals, and it would be true not only for the red diagonal but for all other diagonals. This means that the sums of numbers on every diagonal form the Fibonacci sequence.   ∎

Sierpinski Triangle

Teacher ▷ We give the children a handout of Pascal's triangle with numbers in hexagons. Due to the time-consuming nature of the next problem it should be started in class and finished at home.

Problem 4.11. Sierpinski Triangle. Color all the odd numbers in Pascal's triangle.

The result of the students' work is shown below:

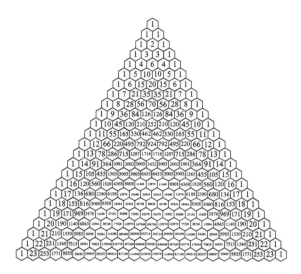

This amazing shape is called the *Sierpinski triangle*. It contains many yellow equilateral triangles of different sizes arranged in a fascinating pattern. Each yellow-sided triangle is made of three identical smaller triangles with white space in the middle. Each of the smaller triangles is also made of three identical triangles with white space in the middle, and so on. The Sierpinski triangle has repeating self-similar patterns and is called a *fractal*.

To investigate what it means that the Sierpinski triangle has a "self-similar" pattern we gave the children two new handouts:

(1) The left picture below is the same as the upper part of the previous picture except the yellow and white hexagons are replaced by black and white circles, respectively.

(2) The triangle on the right picture below has twice more rows. If we shrink the left triangle two times, it would be identical to the upper half of the right triangle.

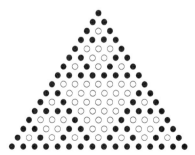
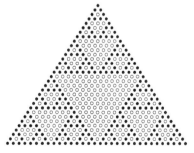

From a distance these two triangles look similar but the second triangle is slightly darker. We asked the children to put the second triangle on top of the first triangle and look through both pages against the bright light. The children observed that each circle of the first triangle contains three circles of the second triangle.

The picture below shows the zoomed-in overlaid triangles that the children studied. For the sake of clarity the black circles in the first triangle are shown in red.

We obtained the Sierpinski triangle by coloring odd numbers in Pascal's triangle or by replacing them with black circles. Can we get the same result in a different way?

Teacher While the following problem is very simple it provides a framework for explaining self-similar patterns in the Sierpinski triangle.

Problem 4.12. Constructing the Sierpinski Triangle with Circles.
The first row of the picture is:

··· ∘ ∘ ∘ ∘ ∘ ∘ ∘ ● ∘ ∘ ∘ ∘ ∘ ∘ ∘ ···

Draw the next seven rows following the modified Pascal's triangle rule: every circle is the sum of two circles above it. The addition rules for the circles are: ∘ + ∘ = ∘, ● + ● = ∘, ● + ∘ = ●, and ∘ + ● = ●.

Almost immediately the students realized that "∘" stands for EVEN numbers, and "●" stands for ODD numbers.

The next few rows were drawn with almost no mistakes. The kids became very excited when they saw the familiar picture of the Sierpinski triangle.

"Why did we get the same picture as the one we obtained by coloring odd numbers in Pascal's triangle?" The kids rushed to answer, "The black circles are in the same places as yellow hexagons since the rules for adding circles are the same as for adding even and odd numbers and we followed the same Pascal's triangle rule." Then we asked, "What will happen if we start with the following line?"

··· ○   ○   ○   ○   ○   ○   ●   ●   ●   ○   ○   ○   ○   ○   ○ ···

Only then the children realized that their argument is incomplete and added, "We started with the line that looks like the first row of Pascal's triangle: one black circle surrounded by white circles."   ■

There are many interesting patterns in the Sierpinski triangle. We asked the children to name some of them. They found quite a few:

- Every black-sided triangle repeats many times in the picture. Some children even said that it would repeat infinitely many times in the "infinite" Pascal's triangle.
- Every black-sided triangle has the same number of black circles on its sides and on its base. That means that these triangles are equilateral.
- Rows 1, 2, 4, 8, 16, 32, and so on consist of black circles only.
- There are "white" upside-down triangles formed by white circles below each row of black circles.
- Every black-sided triangle consists of three smaller black-sided triangles if we agree that one black dot is also a triangle.
- Each black-sided triangle is replicated twice immediately below it.

Many of these observations will be explained in the next problem.

Teacher ▶ We suggest solving the following problem through a guided class discussion.

Problem 4.13. Self-Repeating Patterns in the Sierpinski Triangle. Explain why the Sierpinski triangle has self-repeating patterns. In particular, explain why for each black-sided triangle on the top of the Sierpinski triangle two of its copies are placed side by side immediately below it.

We started with drawing the first four rows of the Sierpinski triangle. These rows contain an equilateral black-sided triangle with side 4:

The class quickly produced the next two rows (they were already drawn in the previous problem). The picture below shows rows 4 and 5:

Since our students have difficulties with general arguments, we insisted they provide a step-by-step explanation of what happens as new rows are added to the picture. Many students needed multiple prompts to come up with explanations similar to the following.

Two black circles in the fifth row are separated by three white circles. Each of these black circles resembles the lonely black circle in the first row. Hence, when more rows are drawn, two black-sided triangles similar to the top one start growing from the two black circles in row 5. In four rows (counting row 5) two new black-sided triangles will be identical to the top one and each will have a black base of length 4. As the Sierpinski triangle grows, its sides and base increase by one circle with each row, so it remains equilateral. In the eighth row the base of the Sierpinski triangle will be 8, which equals the sum of the bases of two new black-sided triangles. Hence, in row 8 the bases of two new black-sided triangles will touch. Now the top black-sided triangle with side 4 together with the two new black-sided triangles form a larger equilateral triangle with side 8 as shown below:

The next row will have two black circles separated by seven white circles. These two black circles are top vertices of two black-sided triangles that would grow in the rows below. They will grow exactly like the top large black-sided triangle until their sides touch. That would happen in row 16 after each of the two black-sided triangles becomes the exact copy of the one on the top: equilateral with sides 8. The bases of these two triangles will form the row of black circles. The resulting picture is shown below:

In the picture above three copies of the black-sided triangles with sides 8 (one on the top and two below) form a black-sided equilateral triangle with sides 16.

"How will the pattern continue? Can you explain it without drawing additional rows?" The kids said that the next row should be of length 17 and contain two black circles separated by 15 white circles. These two black circles would grow into two new black-sided triangles identical to the top 16-row triangle. It takes 16 rows for two new triangles to be completed. Their bases, 16 black circles each, will touch in the 32nd row. Again the top 16-row triangle and two new 16-row triangles form a bigger 32-row triangle. Two new black sided triangles will start to grow in the next row. The kids were convinced that this process could be continued forever, and we did not require any further explanation. ■

Counting Odd and Even Numbers in Pascal's Triangle

The first handout with the Sierpinski triangle consisted of hexagons with numbers that the students colored yellow or left white. These hexagons were then turned into black or white circles. In the next problem we will use hexagons again.

Problem 4.14. Hexagonal Construction Set for the Sierpinski Triangle. Tess wants to assemble yellow and white hexagonal pieces into the Sierpinski triangle.

- How many pieces (both white and yellow) will she need to build the Sierpinski triangle with 16 rows? 32 rows? 64 rows?
- How many yellow pieces will she need for the Sierpinski triangle with 16 rows? 32 rows? 64 rows?

Teacher ▶ The question about 64 rows could be skipped if the students are uncomfortable multiplying and adding large numbers.

The children quickly figured out that Tess will need one hexagon for the first row, two hexagons for the second row, three for the third, and so on. The total number of pieces needed for the first 16 rows is: $1+2+3+\cdots+16$, or the 16th triangular number. Recalling how to compute triangular numbers the students determined that $1 + 2 + 3 + \cdots + 16 = 16 \times 17 \div 2 = 136$.

Similarly the 32nd triangular number is: $1 + 2 + \cdots + 32 = 32 \times 33 \div 2 = 528$ and the 64th is: $1 + 2 + \cdots + 64 = 64 \times 65 \div 2 = 2080$.

To compute the number of yellow hexagons many children drew a 16-row Sierpinski triangle and started counting pieces on the picture.

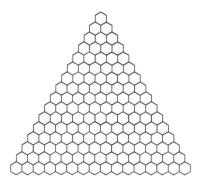

"Can we do it faster?" Hint: "Consider smaller and simpler problems. Start with counting yellow hexagons in 1, 2, 4, and so on top rows."

The kids immediately stated that there is one yellow hexagon in the first row and three in the first two rows. Several children needed another hint to avoid counting hexagons on the picture: "Recall the self-repeating nature of the Sierpinski triangle." Then the class recollected that the 4-row triangle contains three copies of the 2-row triangle with white space in the middle. So, in total there are $3 + 3 + 3 = 3 \times 3 = 9 = 3^2$ yellow hexagons in the first four rows.

In a couple of minutes the kids explained that a triangle with eight rows contains three 4-row triangles. So, it has $9 + 9 + 9 = 3 \times 9 = 3^3 = 27$ yellow hexagons. Continuing in the same way, the students created the following table:

Count of Rows	1	2	4	8	16	32	64
Count of all hexagons	1	3	10	36	136	528	2080
Count of yellow hexagons	1	3	9	27	81	243	720

Problem 4.15. Odd Versus Even Numbers in Pascal's Triangle. Are there more odd or even numbers in the first four rows of Pascal's triangle? the first 16 rows? 64 rows?

Many students remembered that in the previous table the yellow hexagons represented odd numbers. Several students proposed to compute the number of white hexagons that represent even numbers as the total hexagons minus yellow ones. We suggested recording the results in a table. The children quickly filled the fourth row of the following table and noticed that for small triangles more than half of the numbers are odd. However, in a triangle with 64 rows more than half of the numbers is even.

Count of Rows	1	2	4	8	16	32	64
Count of all numbers	1	3	10	36	136	528	2080
Count of odd numbers	1	3	9	27	81	243	729
Count of even numbers	0	0	1	9	55	285	1360
Share of odd numbers	100%	100%	90%	75%	60%	46%	35%

More advanced students decided to compute the share of odd numbers. The results of their computations are shown in the last row of the above table. The students concluded that the share of odd numbers decreases when we consider triangles with more and more rows. Indeed, this is an accurate observation for triangles with the number of rows being a power of 2.

Math Context. The exact behavior of a share of odd numbers in Pascal's triangle is more complicated as shown in the picture below. The count of rows on the horizontal axis starts from 0. The vertical axis shows the share of odd numbers:

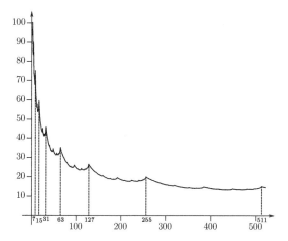

Now let us investigate a completely different way of building the Sierpinski triangle.

Problem 4.16. Pictures with Yellow Triangles. The first two pictures of the sequence are shown below. Draw two more pictures in the sequence following the rule: every △-triangle is replaced by three smaller △-triangles arranged in a triangular formation as in picture 2.

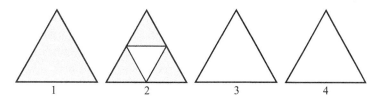

Find the number of △-triangles and ▽-triangles in the 6th picture without drawing it. Compute the total number of yellow triangles in the first two, three, four, five, and six pictures.

The majority of the students were able to draw the third and the fourth pictures without any help from us:

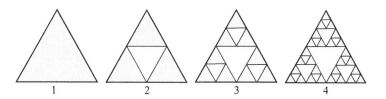

A number of children drew the pictures by dividing the sides of each yellow equilateral triangle in half, connecting these midpoints and getting three yellow and one white triangles instead of each yellow triangle.

Others used a different recipe. First, shrink the previous picture in half in all directions. Then place one copy of the shrunken image on the top of the next picture and two more copies on the bottom, arranging them as yellow triangles in picture 2.

Everybody was very excited to see that the newly created pictures look like the Sierpinski triangle.

Then the children discovered that the number of $\triangle$-triangles triples from picture to picture because each yellow triangle turns into three. They found that there should be $1 \times 3 \times 3 \times 3 \times 3 \times 3 = 243$ yellow triangles in the 6th picture. We recorded this result along with the counts of yellow triangles in the previous pictures in the red row of the table below.

Counting $\triangledown$-triangles was more challenging. Most children noticed that going from picture 2 to picture 3 above, each $\triangle$-triangle turns into one $\triangledown$-triangle and three $\triangle$-triangles. At the same time the white triangle present in Picture 2 remains unchanged. The kids claimed that similar transformations will occur going from the 3rd to the 4th picture, 4th to the 5th pictures and so on. In particular, at each step all the white triangles will remain unchanged and each yellow triangle will be replaced by one white and three yellow triangles. Hence, to determine the number of $\triangledown$-triangles one should look at the previous picture and add the number of $\triangledown$-triangles to the number of $\triangle$-triangles there. This computation is shown in the black row of the table below.

A few students found a different approach: they observed that each picture contains three shrunken copies of the previous picture and one large white triangle in the middle. So, they computed the number of $\triangledown$-triangles as three times the number of $\triangledown$-triangles in the previous picture plus 1.

The total number of yellow triangles in the first picture, first two pictures, first three pictures, and so on, is recorded in the last row of the table below. The children quickly realized that they should fill this row from left to right adding the number of $\triangle$-triangles in the current picture to the previous total. This approach is shown in the blue row:

Picture #	1	2	3	4	5	6
# $\triangle$-triangles per picture	1	1×3 $= 3$	3×3 $= 9$	9×3 $= 27$	27×3 $= 81$	81×3 $= 243$
# $\triangledown$-triangles per picture	0	$0 + 1$ $= 1$	$1 + 3$ $= 4$	$4 + 9$ $= 13$	$13 + 27$ $= 40$	$40 + 81$ $= 121$
Total # $\triangle$-triangles in all pictures	1	$1 + 3$ $= 4$	$4 + 9$ $= 13$	$13 + 27$ $= 40$	$40 + 81$ $= 121$	$121 + 243$ $= 364$

Problem 4.17. Patterns in the Pictures with Yellow Triangles.
Find and explain the patterns in the table above.

We worked on this problem together as a class. The children discovered quite a few patterns. Note that the first three were already explained in the previous problem. For the sake of simplicity we called the total number of △-triangles in all the pictures from the first through the current one (recorded in the last row of the table above) a "running total of △-triangles for the current step".

Pattern 1: The number of △-triangles triples from one picture to the next.

Pattern 2: The number of ▽-triangles is the sum of the numbers of ▽-triangles and △-triangles in the previous picture.

Pattern 3: The number of ▽-triangles is three times the number of ▽-triangles in the previous picture plus 1.

Pattern 4: The running total of △-triangles is three times the running total of △-triangles for the previous step plus 1.

Explanation: The best explanation offered by the kids was based on the rule for generating the next picture from the previous one. To simplify this explanation we helped the kids to draw the pictures below. Going from each triangle in the top row to the triangle in the bottom row, the number of yellow triangles triples as noted in Pattern 2. So, the total number of △-triangles in the bottom row is one (the first triangle on the left) plus three times the total number of △-triangles in the top row.

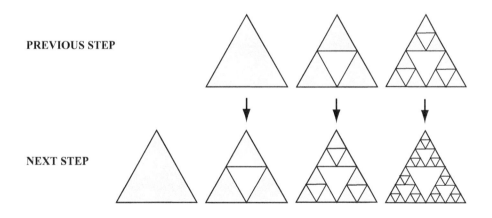

PREVIOUS STEP

NEXT STEP

Pattern 5: The number of ▽-triangles in any given picture is equal to the running total of △-triangles for the previous step.

Explanation: The number of ▽-triangles and the total number of △-triangles follow the same rule: triple the number in the previous picture and add 1. The numbers in these two rows are shifted because the first picture has one △-triangle and zero ▽-triangles.

Pattern 6: The running total of △-triangles for each step is the sum of the number of △-triangles and the number of ▽-triangles for that picture. In other words, every entry in the last row of the table above equals the sum of the two numbers above it.

Explanation: Several students pointed out that this pattern follows from the previous one. The running total of △-triangles at a certain step equals the sum of the number of △-triangles in that picture and the running total of △-triangles for the previous step. The latter is the same as the number of ▽-triangles in the current picture.

Pattern 7: The number of △-triangles in a picture is twice the running total of △-triangles for the previous step plus 1.

Explanation: Many students needed a hint: "Finding pictures 1, 2, and 3 in picture 4 helps to solve the problem."

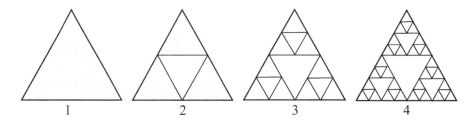

Surprisingly, the children found the solution very quickly, creating the pictures similar to the one below. To get the number of △-triangles on picture 4, one should add twice the number of △-triangles on picture 3 (circled green), twice the number of △-triangles on picture 2 (circled blue), twice the number of △-triangles on picture 1 (circled red), and one. The latter accounts for the top △-triangle circled purple.

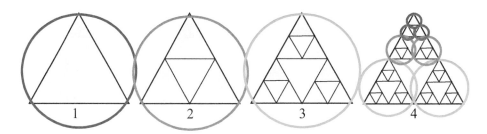

The children were sure that the same arguments work for all other pictures.   ◼

Pascal's Triangle Modulo 3

Teacher ▶ It is helpful to review the division of integers modulo 3 discussed in detail in Chapter 3, "Fibonacci Numbers", before the next problem.

We give the children a handout of Pascal's triangle with circled numbers.

Problem 4.18. Color Pascal's Triangle Modulo 3. Color Pascal's triangle as follows:

- Leave white the circles with numbers that are divisible by 3.
- Color blue the circles with numbers that have remainder 1 when divided by 3.
- Color red the circles with numbers that have remainder 2 when divided by 3.

Find as many patterns as you can in the obtained picture.

The children quickly discovered that trying to divide numbers in Pascal's triangle by 3 and compute remainders is not a good way to solve this problem. Instead, they decided to create rules for addition of white, blue, and red circles similar to the rules used for the black and white circles in Problem 4.12. Pretty soon the students realized that they need to translate the table for addition of remainders mod 3 from Chapter 3, "Fibonacci Numbers", to colors:

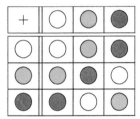

Many children found using this table confusing when they worked on coloring Pascal's triangle. So, we recommended creating a "cheat sheet" of answers for adding two colors according to the Pascal's triangle rule:

Looking at the "cheat sheet" several children commented, "White circles act as zeros. Also, since adding two circles of different colors, blue and red, gives a white circle, blue and red circles act like 1 and -1." Indeed, since $2 + 1$ equals 0 modulo 3, then 2 equals -1 modulo 3.

The students proceeded to color their handouts and produced the following beautiful picture:

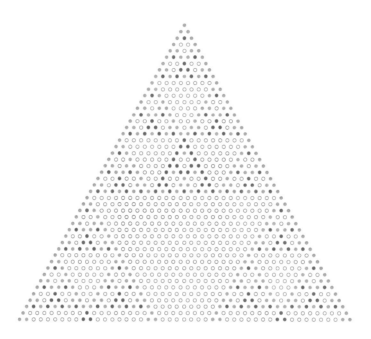

The children discovered the following patterns illustrated on the picture below:

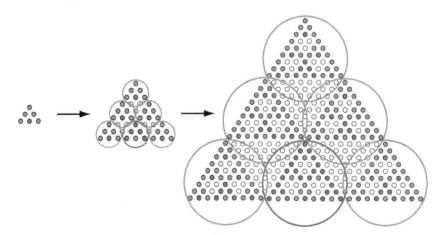

- The top 3-row triangle (left picture above) is formed by six dots: five blue and one red.
- The top 9-row triangle (middle picture above) is formed by six 3-row triangles. Five of 3-row triangles (shown inside the blue circles) are copies of the top 3-row triangle on the left picture. These copies are arranged as blue dots of the top 3-row triangle. The sixth 3-row triangle (shown inside the red circle and positioned as the red dot of the top

3-row triangle) is obtained from the top 3-row triangle by turning blue dots into red and red dots into blue. The spaces between the six 3-row triangles are filled with white dots. These white dots form equilateral triangles.

- The top 27-row triangle (right picture above) is formed by six 9-row triangles. Five of the 9-row triangles (shown inside blue circles) are copies of the top 9-row triangle. These copies are arranged as blue dots of the top 3-row triangle (left picture above). The sixth 9-row triangle (shown inside a red circle and positioned as the red dot of the top 3-row triangle) is obtained from the top 9-row triangle by switching blue and red dots. The spaces between the six 9-row triangles are filled with white dots. These white dots form equilateral triangles.

The children were convinced that this pattern continues forever: the top 81-row triangle would be made of six 27-row triangles, five of which would be identical to the top 27-row triangle and one would have blue and red dots switched; the top 243-row triangle would be made of six 81-row triangles, and so on. We agreed with this conclusion but decided not to explain it because the explanation is both tedious and difficult for the kids. ■

Chapter 5

Area

We asked our students, "What does the word *area* mean?" One child immediately replied, "I know what area is. It means Bay Area: we all live in the Bay Area."

Teacher In our classes students make all their drawings (except for a few special cases) on graph paper, and the teachers use a grid drawn on the board. Almost all the shapes we consider have corners on the grid, which means that their vertices are on the intersections of vertical and horizontal lines of the grid. We call little grid squares tiles in order to avoid confusion between grid squares and other squares discussed in this chapter. The teacher should be ready to deal with two issues that often arise while teaching this topic to young children:

- Instead of using the grid in the notebooks, the children draw their own grid on top of the existing one.
- Our pictures on the board are imperfect, and we instruct the students to imagine "the same but perfect" pictures in their minds. Still, sometimes the children are confused about which imperfections are intentional and which must be fixed.

Playing with Squares

Teacher Since an accurate definition of area as a number is tricky and we believe that introducing it in our classes is counterproductive, we do not use the term "area" until the children have some experience with it. Instead, the following problems let kids play with this concept without mentioning the term.

Problem 5.1. Fold the Square. Fold the square shown below.

- The result should be a square.
- It should have two layers of paper everywhere.

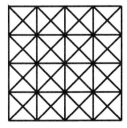

The above square has a lot of extra slanted lines, which help the younger children to solve the problem. For older children one can simply use a square piece of paper.

At first, many children solved this problem incorrectly. Some of them folded the square along the vertical or horizontal midline getting a rectangle, not a square, with two layers of paper everywhere. Others folded the square twice, first along the vertical midline, and then along the horizontal midline, getting a square with four layers everywhere.

Once the children realized their mistakes, most finished the problem fairly quickly:

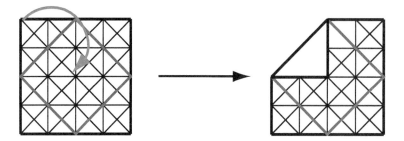

Problem 5.2. Baby Goat. A baby goat eats all the grass from the field shown below in one day. Draw a square field with corners on the grid that can feed the baby goat for two days.

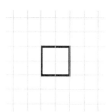

Many children started counting tiles, discovered that the field sufficient for two days should consist of eight tiles, and concluded that the problem has no solution since 8 is not a square number. We had to assure them that such a square exists.

Despite discussing this problem in great detail, some of our students repeated the same mistake in the next few problems: they kept claiming that there are no squares with corners on the grid and with the number of tiles that is not a square number.

Among other wrong answers, a 4×2 rectangle and a 3×3 square were the most popular.

To get the solution some students needed a hint: "Think about the 'Fold the Square' problem." Finally, the class got the desired solution: the field sufficient for two days is shown in red.

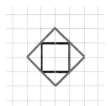

Many children thought that the shape of the field sufficient for two days is called a diamond. Indeed, a square or rhombus rotated so that one corner is pointing down is sometimes called a diamond. We prefer not to use the word diamond when discussing mathematics since it is too confusing. It stresses one rarely important aspect — how the shape is rotated, and obscures the really important one — that the shape is a square or a rhombus. We demonstrated it by cutting a square out of paper and gradually rotating it in front of the class while asking, "Is it still a square? When does it become a diamond?" Some students still weren't convinced, so we took one of their name tags, John's, and asked while rotating it, "Is it still John? Or is it now somebody else?" Everybody laughed, and we hope would remember that if the shape is a square, it remains a square no matter how it is positioned.

Problem 5.3. Waffles. A hungry math circle teacher chooses between two small waffles shown below on the left or one waffle on the right. All pieces are of the same thickness. Help the teacher to get a bigger portion without counting tiles in any of the waffles.

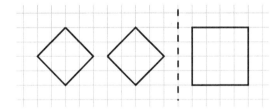

Several children ignored part of the requirements and found the correct answer (two choices are equivalent) by counting tiles. We had to remind them that they were supposed to find a solution without counting tiles. In a few minutes the class proposed three different methods.

Some students decided to cut the left small waffle along the diagonals into four equal triangular pieces. Then they built the large waffle out of the whole small waffle and four triangular pieces.

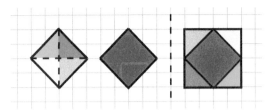

Alternatively, a few kids cut each small waffle along one of its diagonals into two triangular pieces and built a new waffle out of them.

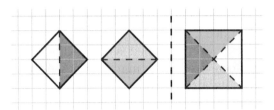

A number of children recognized that they could fold the big waffle the same way as in the "Fold the Square" problem. The result consisted of two layers, with each layer equal to the smaller waffle on the left.

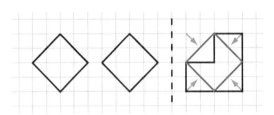

Problem 5.4. Goat. A goat eats all the grass on a 3×3 grass field in one day. Draw a square field with corners on the grid that can feed the goat for two days.

A few students attempted to solve the problem similarly to the "Baby Goat" problem (see the left picture below). We asked these students, "Are the corners of the new square on the grid?" In response, some of them corrected their answer by moving the bigger square half of a tile diagonally. One possible outcome is shown on the right:

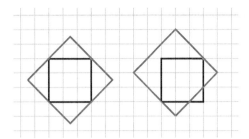

We wanted the children to see how this problem can be reduced to the "Fold the Square" problem. So we stated an additional requirement: "The field sufficient for two days must share two corners with the one-day field." At the same time we gave a hint: "It might be helpful to draw a four-day square field."

The students drew the picture below without any difficulties. The field sufficient for the goat for four days is shown as a big dashed square, and the two-day field is shown in red.

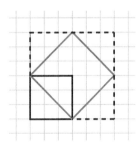

Finally, we were ready to introduce the term *"area"*. What does this term mean? The children explained that area is the amount of space inside a shape. We agreed and pointed out that this space is paper in the "Fold the Square" problem, a grass field in the "Baby Goat" and "Goat" problems, or a waffle in the "Waffles" problem.

Areas of Similar Shapes

Problem 5.5. Greedy Goat. A greedy goat eats all the grass on a square field in one day. She asks her Fairy Goat Mother to double the sides of this good-for-one-day field (both length and width). How many days would it take the goat to eat the grass on the new field?

Then the greedy goat asks the Fairy Goat Mother to increase the length and width of the good-for-one-day field 3 times; 4 times; 5 times; 8 times. Find the pattern for the number of days it would take the goat to eat the grass on the new fields.

The students began drawing square fields produced by the Fairy Goat Mother and counting tiles, but after one or two pictures they recognized the pattern of square numbers discussed in Chapter 1, "Numbers as Geometric Shapes". The children quickly squared the sides of the new fields and got the number of days it would take the goat to eat the grass on those fields:

Side	1	2	3	4	5	8
Days	1	4	9	16	25	64

This is a good opportunity to clarify that the word "size" that children often use when talking about area and length creates ambiguity. There is no correct answer to the question: "Is 'the size' of the largest field in the previous problem 8 or 64 times larger than the original field?" To avoid ambiguity one must always use the specific words *area* or *side*.

Teacher ➤ In the classes for the advanced students the first part of the problem below may be restated as a hint for the second part of the problem.

Problem 5.6. Valentine Goat. A Valentine goat eats all the grass on a heart-shaped field in one day.

Her Fairy Goat Mother doubles the length and width of the grass field. How many days would it take the goat to eat the grass on the new field?

What happens if the field has the following shape?

Almost immediately the children realized that if the field is made of little square pieces, it doesn't matter how many little squares it contains. As the field increases the area of each square quadruples and the entire field would be sufficient for four days.

Then the kids explained that doubling the length and width of the red heart-shaped field would also turn it into a field sufficient for four days. The majority just stated that it is analogous to the model field. We considered such an intuitive explanation sufficient since the accurate one is too complicated for our students.

Surprisingly, a student or two went further and almost came up with the full explanation. They proposed splitting the heart-shaped field into a number of squares and the "curvy pieces", then splitting the "curvy pieces" into smaller squares and smaller remaining "curvy pieces", then repeating the process a couple more times. They explained that the remaining tiny "curvy pieces" won't matter and the rest consists of squares with different sides. Areas of all these squares quadruple and so does the area of the entire field.

In conclusion, everybody agreed that the shape of the original field does not affect the result. ∎

Teacher Before posing the next problem we recalled how we used "pseudo-languages" to establish isomorphisms in Problems 3.2 and 3.3 from Chapter 3, "Fibonacci Numbers". If you don't want to use this trick, you may want to change the next problem as follows: We have a bag of small equilateral triangles with sides 1. How many such triangles should be used to tile an equilateral triangle with sides 3? Formulate a problem about the hungry goat eating grass on a triangular field that is isomorphic ("the same") to this problem.

Problem 5.7. Translating From "Tilean" Language. Sasha's room is an equilateral triangle with sides 3. She tiled the floor using the tiles in the shape of equilateral triangles with sides 1. Find how many such tiles she used by translating this problem into "Valentine-Goatean" language of the previous problem.

Several of the students tiled the room and recalled that this problem was already solved using two different methods in Chapter 1, "Numbers as Geometric Shapes" (Problems 1.7 and 1.18).

We insisted on a solution based on translation. The students who figured out how to do it became very excited and eager to explain that a single tile should be turned into the goat's initial field sufficient for one day. Since 3 units = 3×1 unit, the Fairy Goat Mother should triple the sides of the initial field. Then the number of tiles is the same as the number of days the goat would graze on the large field. Thus, the children arrived at the following translation:

The Valentine goat had a triangular field with enough grass for one day. Her Fairy Goat Mother increased the length and width of the field 3 times. How many days would it take the goat to eat all the grass on the large field?

From the previous two problems ("Greedy Goat" and "Valentine Goat") we already know that it is $3^2 = 3 \times 3 = 9$. This provides yet another explanation of why tiling an equilateral triangle with tiles of the same shape requires a square number of tiles. ∎

Teacher In the next problem we need to divide fractions with numerator 1 in half, however, many young children have difficulties using fractions. To help these kids we say, "If one needs eight slices to make the whole pizza, we write that the size of one slice is $\frac{1}{8}$." Then we discuss what happens with pieces of pizza when we repeatedly divide them in half, "What is one half of $\frac{1}{2}$, one half of $\frac{1}{4}$, and one half of $\frac{1}{8}$?"

The pictures for the next problem should be drawn without the grid to eliminate the idea of counting tiles.

Problem 5.8. ABCDE Squares. Ann draws a black square with side 1. Bob joins the midpoints of its sides and gets a red square. Then Carl does the same with Bob's square, Deb with Carl's square, and Eva with Deb's. Their squares are blue, green, and orange:

Fill in the empty cells in the table below.

	Ann	Bob	Carl	Deb	Eva
Area					
Side	1	—		—	

A few children needed a hint: "Recall the 'Fold the Square' problem (Problem 5.1)." Soon everyone determined that the area of Bob's square is $\frac{1}{2}$ of the area of Ann's square. Also, the area of Carl's square is $\frac{1}{2}$ of the area of Bob's square. So it is $\frac{1}{4}$ of the area of Ann's square. The students continued in the same manner and finished the area row:

Name	Ann	Bob	Carl	Deb	Eva
Area	1	$\frac{1}{2}$	$\frac{1}{4}$	$\frac{1}{8}$	$\frac{1}{16}$
Side	1	—		—	

While many kids were able to finish the problem on their own, the rest needed additional help. As a hint we drew the left picture on the board:

The class recognized that the area of the yellow square is $\frac{1}{4}$ of the area of the black square. They matched the black square with Ann's square, and the yellow square with Carl's square. They concluded that the side of Carl's square is $\frac{1}{2}$ of the side of Ann's square.

A number of students explained that in two steps the side decreases two times. Therefore, Eva's side is $\frac{1}{2}$ of Carl's side and $\frac{1}{4}$ of Ann's side. Other students drew a picture for Eva's square (above on the right). They noticed that one needs 16 copies of the green square to cover the large square and the side of the green square is $\frac{1}{4}$ of the side of the large square. Finally, the whole table was filled:

Name	Ann	Bob	Carl	Deb	Eva
Area	1	$\frac{1}{2}$	$\frac{1}{4}$	$\frac{1}{8}$	$\frac{1}{16}$
Side	1	—	$\frac{1}{2}$	—	$\frac{1}{4}$

∎

Teacher ▷ The children are often eager to extend the table by making the squares smaller and smaller. Surprisingly, in this context even the first and second graders were writing such monstrous fractions as $\frac{1}{256}$ without hesitation.

A few kids were curious about what happens in the case of cross-out cells. We explained that those answers cannot be written as fractions.

SAME SHAPE SAME SIZE

The children know that when a geometric figure is moved, it does not change its shape and size. This allows us to say that two shapes are *SAME SHAPE SAME SIZE* if we can find a way to overlay them, so that they coincide. The concept of SAME SHAPE SAME SIZE is so important in geometry that mathematicians have a special name for it: *congruent* [3].

Teacher ▷ Many children may not be comfortable with the word congruent and, once they forget what it means, there is no way to recall the meaning. Hence, we use the words SAME SHAPE SAME SIZE instead. The reason we mention the word "congruent" is to prepare the children in case they see or hear it elsewhere. Also, some children are fascinated by new words.

The next problem is very simple, but it introduces a new concept, so we offered it as a class discussion.

Problem 5.9. SAME SHAPE SAME SIZE? Which of the shapes below have the same shape, which have the same area, and which are SAME SHAPE SAME SIZE?

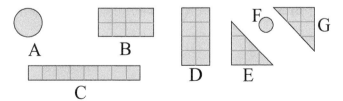

The children immediately answered that the circles A and F have the same shape but their areas are different. Rectangles B and C have the same area 8 but are not SAME SHAPE SAME SIZE. Rectangles B and D and triangles E and G are SAME SHAPE SAME SIZE. The children explained that if we cut out these shapes, we can find a way to put one on top of the other so that they coincide.   ■

Problem 5.10. Rocket. Draw a rectangle of the same area as the rocket below.

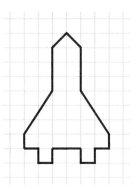

The children began computing the area by dividing the rocket into a number of rectangles and squares of total area 20, the rocket's nose, and the wings. They easily determined that the nose has area 1 but stumbled on the triangular rocket wings. After some pondering they figured out that the wings can be joined together to form a 2×3 rectangle. The total area of the rocket is $20 + 1 + 6 = 27$, and there are two rectangles of area 27: 3×9 and 1×27.   ■

Teacher ▶ Unlike in Chapter 1, "Numbers as Geometric Shapes", in this chapter we consider as different only the shapes that are not congruent.

Problem 5.11. Area of a Right Triangle. Calculate the area of each of the following right triangles. Propose the general procedure.

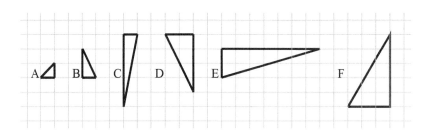

Teacher ▶ Many students do not need so many easy examples to figure out how to compute the area of a right triangle. We ask them to find areas of triangles B, C, and E only, and then to state the general method.

The children immediately found the areas of the first two triangles, $\frac{1}{2}$ and 1. Many of them found the area of the second triangle by cutting it along the horizontal midline and rearranging pieces to form one tile. They tried the same approach for the third triangle but could not get the answer. Hint: "Recall the wings of the rocket." The children completed the third triangle to a rectangle shown by dashed lines below, and realized that the rectangle consists of two triangles that are SAME SHAPE SAME SIZE. So, the area of the original triangle must be half of the area of the rectangle: $5 \div 2 = 2\frac{1}{2}$. Then, the students easily found the areas of all the remaining triangles: 4, 7, and $7\frac{1}{2}$.

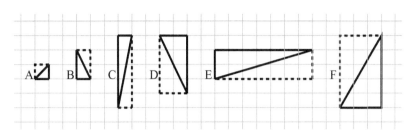

Finally, the class came up with the general procedure. To find the area of any right triangle one should:

- Draw a rectangular frame about the right triangle (shown above using dashed lines).
- Find the area of the framing rectangle.
- The area of the right triangle is half of the area of the framing rectangle. ∎

Rotation by a Right Angle

Teacher▷ The majority of the children do not know that to determine a particular rotation one has to specify its center, angle, and direction. Instead of defining these terms we introduce them through the following problems.

Problem 5.12. Smiley Faces. What happened to the first square (on the left) when it became the second, or the third, or the fourth square in the picture below? We assume that the square is rotated "in place".

Our students had no problem determining the direction of the rotation above, but instead of using words, such as counterclockwise, they used gestures, turning their hands as if rotating a square and saying that the square was "flipped" or "turned". However, "flip" is not the right word to use because it describes a three-dimensional movement that shows the back side of the page. The word "turn" has too many different meanings. Since the word *rotation* is traditionally used in mathematics, we will use it from now on.

"How far should we rotate the first square to get the second one?" The children gave two versions of the same answer: 90° or right angle.

"What is a 90° or right angle?" The most popular answer was that it's an angle formed by horizontal and vertical lines. A tilted right angle drawn on the board showed that this definition doesn't work.

To clarify the notion of the right angle rotation we gave the following demonstration: the teacher stands facing the class with arms extended and clasped together pointing to the class, as an arrow in a wind vane.

"Where will the arms point after the right angle rotation?" The children explained that the answer depends on whether the teacher turns left or right. At this time we introduced the words "clockwise" and "counterclockwise" rotations.

The next two questions presented no difficulties for the students: "How many right angle rotations does it take for the arms to point to the board (with teacher's back turned to the class)? How many right angle rotations does it take for the arms to return to the initial position, to complete the full circle?"

Returning to the starting position is the only rotation that can be described precisely since the starting point is the exact position. This rotation is called *full rotation* and by convention it is assigned a measure of 360°. Now the children were able to describe the right angle rotation as a quarter of the full rotation; it is $360° \div 4 = 90°$. From now on it is appropriate to use 90° and *right angle* interchangeably.

"What is a 1° angle?" The children explained that a 1° angle is $\frac{1}{90}$ of the right angle and some children yelled that it is also $\frac{1}{360}$ of the full angle.

Returning to the "Smiley Faces" problem, the children were able to use precise words, "The square was repeatedly rotated counterclockwise by 90° or clockwise by 270°."

This description is still insufficient as we will find out in the next problem. We will finish the current problem after the next one.

Problem 5.13. Rotating a Rectangle. Take a rigid rectangular object (for example, a piece of cardboard) and place it on the board. In how many ways can it be rotated by 90°?

Initially the children answered that there are two ways: clockwise and counterclockwise. We decided to count only clockwise rotations, and the children's answer changed to one. Then we asked four students to come to the board and show this one rotation.

When the first child was rotating the rectangle shown in black in the top left picture below, we held it (pressing it to the board) at the upper left corner and traced the result in red. For the second child we returned the rectangle to its original position and held it at the upper right corner (the top right picture below). The majority of children did not notice the switch of the point we held and were surprised to see a different result. For the third and the fourth child we held the rectangle at the lower right and lower left corners, respectively (the bottom left and right pictures). At this point the majority of the children figured out our trick and were convinced that the total number of clockwise rotations is four since the rectangle has four corners.

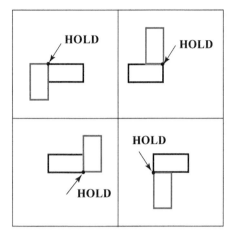

"Must we hold a rectangle at a corner?" The children shouted, "No!" and some figured out the correct answer to the original problem, "infinity". To help the rest of the class, we called the fifth child to the board and she rotated the rectangle about its center.

Now everybody realized that there are infinitely many clockwise rotations by 90°. Indeed, the rectangle can be rotated about any point, called the *center of rotation*, and the final position of the rectangle depends on the choice of this point.   ■

Returning to the "Smiley Faces" problem, the children were able to identify the center of rotation as the center of the square (the missing nose in the smiley face). However, surprisingly, many of them could not point it out correctly. Hint: "One can find the center of rotation by drawing two lines. Which lines?" The students responded, "The center of rotation is at the intersection of the diagonals of the square."   ■

Problem 5.14. Folding Fairy. In Fairyland sheets of paper have irregular shape:

A Fairy wants to fold this piece of paper to get a right angle. Give her instructions, and she will follow them word by word. Then give the Fairy instructions to obtain 45° and 135° angles.

The first part of the problem should be solved in two steps: creating a straight edge and making the right angle. While each step by itself is trivial for the kids, only a few children found the solution right away; many did not realize the two-step nature of the problem and needed a hint: "Can you solve the problem if the paper has a straight edge?" Soon everyone produced the right angle:

The exact positions of the folding lines (shown above as blue dashed lines) do not matter.

The children obtained the 45° angle in no time by folding the right angle in half. The children did not realize that strictly speaking this recipe does not work since it is not possible to guarantee that the new folding line passes through the corner. We decided not to bring their attention to this defect.

Many kids struggled with the 135° angle. Finally, they figured out that 135° = 180° − 45° and produced the 135° angle by partially unfolding the 45° angle.   ■

Teacher ➤ In the beginning of the next problem we reminded children what the words "right triangle", "leg", and "hypotenuse" mean.

Problem 5.15. Triangles in a Square. Describe which rotation moves the green triangle onto the blue one.

The children, who couldn't solve the problem in a few minutes, needed a hint: "What would happen with the square after the described rotation?" Many students noticed that the rotated square needs to coincide with the original one. Almost all of them could determine the magnitude of the rotation: a counterclockwise rotation by 90° or a clockwise by 270°. Yet many of the children had to be reminded that one needs to find the center of rotation too. Then the kids realized that the square is rotated about its center, similarly to the "Smiley Faces" problem.   ■

Problem 5.16. More Triangles in a Square. Repeat the rotation discussed in the previous problem. Draw the positions of the green triangle after all possible repeated rotations. What new shape do you see? Why?

Drawing the results of the repeated rotation turned out to be a very challenging exercise for some of our students. To help them we highlighted the legs of the green triangle differently.

As soon as they got the correct picture shown above, several children yelled, "We got a square in the middle!" Others disagreed; they were convinced that it cannot be a square. We asked the class, "Why do you think it is or is not a square?"

Teacher ▶ Many children do not understand that the last question is equivalent to finding a way to check that a shape is a square. To prepare children for this discussion we gave them warmup Problem 6.14 about squares a few weeks earlier.

"How can we check that a shape is a square?" Usually the children reply very quickly, "We should check that all sides of the quadrilateral are equal." However, the shape below is a quadrilateral with all equal sides but it is not a square. This shape is called a *rhombus*.

The next answer we commonly get is that a square is a quadrilateral with all sides equal and four right angles. This answer is correct but specifying the magnitude of all the angles is excessive, there is a simpler definition that is easier to check. Hint: "What did we require about the sides? What about the angles?" Finally, several children realized that it is enough to require that all the angles are equal. So, a square is a quadrilateral with all sides equal and all angles equal.

At last, we were ready to look again at the red quadrilateral obtained by repeated rotations and discuss whether it is a square. The children explained that it is a square because:

- All sides are equal since they are the results of the rotations of the same side of the green triangle.
- Showing the equality of all angles is more challenging and we heard several different explanations. Some observed that each rotation moves one angle of the red quadrilateral onto its other angle, which means that all angles are equal. Others showed the equality of all angles by considering the rotated triangle. Since the green triangle is rotated

onto the blue one, the angles of the green triangle are equal to the corresponding angles of the blue triangle. Similar observations can be made for the other triangles. To visualize the students' argument we colored the corresponding equal acute angles of all triangles using purple and yellow colors (see the picture below). Now, each angle of the red quadrilateral together with two acute angles (purple and yellow) form a straight 180° angle. This means that all angles of the red quadrilateral are equal.

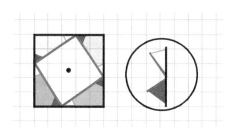

Math Context. We have just shown that any quadrilateral with a symmetry of the right angle rotation is a square.

Area of a Tilted Square

Teacher In the following discussion we use the words "straight square" to reference the squares with sides on the grid, and the words "tilted square" otherwise.

Problem 5.17. Area of a Tilted Square. Find the area of the red quadrilateral below. Do not draw anything else in the picture and do not count tiles.

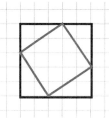

The red shape above was familiar to the kids from the previous problem, and there was no need to discuss why this shape is a square.

Disregarding our request not to draw any lines on the picture a number of kids found the area of the "tilted" square by splitting it into four triangles and a square. They called the splitted square a "propeller" (see the picture below on the left). We asked these students, "Have you drawn any additional lines on the picture?"

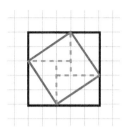 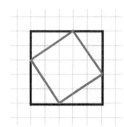

In a few minutes many students discovered that the area of the red square equals the area of the big black square, $5 \times 5 = 25$, minus the area of the four yellow triangles (see the right picture above). The area of each triangle is 3 since it is half of the area of the 2×3 rectangle. Therefore, the area of the red tilted square is $25 - 3 \times 4 = 25 - 12 = 13$. ■

Problem 5.18. Area of Another Tilted Square. Find the area of the red quadrilateral shown below on the left. Do not draw anything else in the picture and do not count tiles.

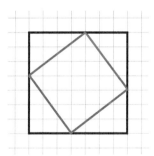 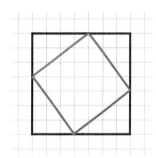

First, we used this opportunity to let our students repeat the arguments which show that the red quadrilateral is a square (see Problem 5.16).

Then, they easily found its area by removing the yellow triangles of area $4 \times 3 \div 2 = 6$ from the 7×7 black square (see the right picture above): $49 - 4 \times 6 = 25$. ■

We asked the class, "What is the side of the red square above?" The children could not believe their calculations. Many were convinced that only a straight square could have side 5. A few kids even thought that the side of the red square is $3 + 4 = 7$.

Problem 5.19. Four Tables. Imagine that the 5×5 square below is a room, and the four colored triangles are four triangular tables. The red tilted square is a free space in that room. Move the tables in the room so that the free space consists of two squares. There are two such arrangements of the tables; find both.

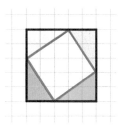

Teacher This problem is difficult for many younger students. We gave these children scissors and handouts with two copies of the picture above, advising them to cut out the tables in one room to rearrange them in the other.

The majority of the children found the arrangement similar to the one shown below on the left first. It is obtained by moving the bottom green table next to the top green table and the bottom blue table next to the top blue table. Then the free space consists of two squares. To see these squares one needs to draw an additional dashed line. Finding the second arrangement (shown on the right) turned out to be more challenging. It is obtained from the first arrangement by sliding the entire blue rectangle down.

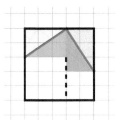 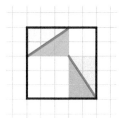

Problem 5.20. Four Tables in the Land of Giants. Giants use triangular tables with sides 250 and 350:

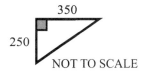

- Can the giants put such triangular tables into the corners of a square room so that the tables touch the same way as in the statement of the previous problem?
- What is the side of this square room?
- Is the free space in this room a square?
- Find two ways to move the tables so that the free space becomes two squares.

Teacher To avoid anxiety about regular graph paper being too small we insisted on using paper without grids for this problem.

While most of the children easily drew the solution, some children needed a hint: "Recall what the side of the room was in the previous problem. What should it be now?" The children replied, "In the Land of Giants it should be $250 + 350 = 600$."

When the triangular tables are arranged as shown on the left picture below, the free space in the middle is a square. To explain this, the students rotated the square as in Problem 5.16, "More Triangles in a Square".

To transform the free space into two squares, the tables should be moved as shown in the middle and right pictures below:

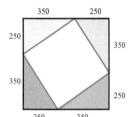 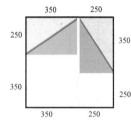 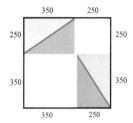

Even the children who found the solution effortlessly did not perceive that in this problem one should explain why the resulting arrangements have no overlaps or gaps between the tables. Once we pointed this out many kids were able to finish the problem. Some of them drew a yellow line as shown on the middle and right pictures above, and explained that the green rectangle touches the line on the left while the blue one touches it on the right. ■

Problem 5.21. Four Supergiant Tables. In the Land of Supergiants even larger tables are used. They are still right triangles, all of the same size, but we do not know exactly how large they are.

- Supergiants need to put four tables into corners of a square room, and they need the free space to be a square. Can they build such a square room?
- Can they rearrange the tables so that the free space becomes two squares?

Many children immediately said, "The sizes of the tables do not matter. The pictures would look the same as for the giant tables." We did not require a full explanation since we knew that the children have problems with statements involving unknown quantities. ■

"What happens to the amount of free space in a room when one moves furniture around?" — "It does not change!" We will call this "the universal law of free space". Now recall all square rooms with four triangular tables that were rearranged in the earlier problems. According to "the universal law of free space" *the area of the big tilted square always equals the sum of the areas of two smaller straight squares.* Soon we will have a special name for this fact. For now, let us use it to solve the following problems.

Problem 5.22. Squares with Areas from 1 to 10. Can one draw a square (straight or tilted) with corners on the grid and of area 1, 2, 3, 4, 5, 6, 7, 8, 9, or 10?

Our students immediately answered, "We know how to draw squares with areas 1, 4, and 9!" A few kids even remembered that we already got squares of areas 2 and 8 as well. Recalling the "Fold the Square" problem they drew those squares (red squares below):

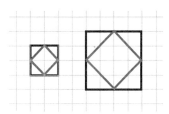

The kids did not know how to approach the remaining cases. They could not relate the current problem to the rule stated above: "the area of the tilted square always equals the sum of the areas of two straight squares". To simplify the problem we started with a familiar case of the square of area 13. Hint: "Have you seen the picture below? It helps to draw the square of area 13."

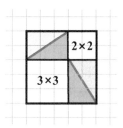

A number of students recognized the picture above as the final result in Problem 5.19, "Four Tables". In that problem the two white squares represented the free space in the room after the triangular tables were re-arranged. Still, a few students needed another hint: "What was the shape of the free space before the tables were moved? Return the tables back to the starting position." With the help of this hint the class arrived at the following familiar picture:

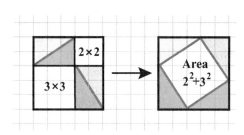

Now several kids were able to draw the squares with areas 5 and 10. Others needed yet another hint: "Using the pictures above as an example, draw the 'tilted' square of area 5." The children presented 5 as $5 = 2^2 + 1^2$ and replaced triangles with legs 3 and 2 (see picture above) by triangles with legs 2 and 1:

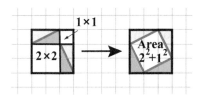

Even though the children were able to draw the correct "tilted" square, most did it by analogy, without fully understanding all the steps. Therefore, we decided to discuss these steps, and helped the class to formulate them:

- Represent 5 as a sum of two squares: $5 = 2^2 + 1^2$. The free space in the rearranged room with four triangular tables is made of these two straight squares.
- Draw the rearranged room and mark two straight squares (2×2 and 1×1) and four triangular tables in it. Note that the side of the room should equal the sum of the sides of two straight squares.
- Move the triangular tables in the room so that the free space becomes one tilted square. That square has the desired area.

Finally, everybody was able to draw the square of area 10. The kids represented 10 as $10 = 3^2 + 1^2$ and drew the left picture below. The tilted square of the required area was obtained by moving the triangular tables (picture below on the right):

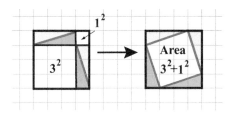

We pointed out that the squares with areas 2 and 8 could also be constructed using the same procedure ($2 = 1^2 + 1^2$ and $8 = 2^2 + 2^2$).

The children tried to draw the squares of areas 3, 6, or 7 with corners on the grid, but couldn't get them. Soon most of the class decided that such squares do not exist. Why? First, numbers 3, 6, and 7 are not square numbers. So, if there were squares of areas 3, 6, or 7 with corners on the grid, they must be "tilted". Then, according to "the universal law of free space", these numbers have to be sums of two square numbers. There are only three square numbers less than 10: 1, 4, and 9. None of 3, 6, and 7 can be obtained by adding two of them. As a result, only squares of areas 1, 2, 4, 5, 8, 9, or 10 can be drawn with corners on the grid. ■

Problem 5.23. Squares with Areas from 11 to 30. Can one draw a square (straight or tilted) with corners on the grid and area 11, 12, 13, ..., 30?

The children immediately found two straight squares of areas 16 and 25. Then, they figured out that if a number can be written as a sum of two squares, a tilted square of such an area can be drawn following the procedure outlined in the previous problem. Since $13 = 4 + 9$, $17 = 16 + 1$, $18 = 9 + 9$, $20 = 16 + 4$, $26 = 25 + 1$, and $29 = 25 + 4$, there are tilted squares with areas 13, 17, 18, 20, 26, and 29.

Explaining why other squares could not be drawn was much more difficult for the students. There are too many possible summands (areas of the straight squares) to consider and the children were losing track of them. We suggested filling in the following addition table:

	1	**4**	**9**	**16**	**25**
1	2	5	10	17	26
4	5	8	13	20	29
9	10	13	18	25	34
16	17	20	25	32	41
25	26	29	34	41	50

The numbers in the top row and the left column (in bold) are the areas of straight squares. The numbers in the other cells are the sums of the top and the left entries; they are the areas of all possible tilted squares (for areas up to 50). For example, the intersection of the column "4" with row "9" is the area $4 + 9 = 13$ of the tilted square we discussed earlier. The kids concluded that if a number is not in any of the cells of the table above, neither straight nor tilted squares with such an area can be drawn with corners on the grid. ■

Pythagorean Theorem

In the preceding problems we used the fact that the area of a tilted square with corners on the grid may be presented as a sum of the areas of two certain straight squares. This fact is called the *Pythagorean theorem*. This famous theorem has been known for at least 2,500 years. Most likely, it was known even before Pythagoras.[1]

Most students who had heard about the Pythagorean theorem knew that it is somehow related to a right triangle. Let us find this triangle in the familiar pictures below:

---

[1] The handout with Pythagoras's biography can be found on page 165.

"Which of the four triangles shares a side with all three white squares?" The kids replied, "On the left the legs of the dark green triangle are sides of two straight squares and on the right the hypotenuse of the dark green triangle is a side of a tilted square."

Let us move the red square from the right picture above to the left picture above, obtaining the left picture below. After removing all the distracting details we get the right picture below:

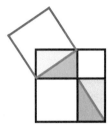 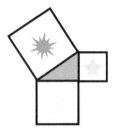

Using the moon, the star, and the sun to denote the areas of the squares, we restated the Pythagorean theorem as:

☀ =   + ✦.

The Pythagorean theorem was studied in schools for centuries, and about two hundred years ago somebody decided that the slightly rotated picture shown above looks like pants. Nowadays many people refer to it as "Pythagoras's pants". Adding a few ornaments makes the picture more memorable:

Very often a few students tell us, "The Pythagorean theorem states that $a^2 + b^2 = c^2$." Usually these kids do not understand how this formula is related to the picture above. Hint: "What expression on the board is similar to $c^2 = a^2 + b^2$?" The children immediately answered that c^2 is the sun, while a^2 and b^2 stand for the moon and the star.

We restated their answer in a more formal way. Let the legs of a right triangle be a and b, and its hypotenuse be c.

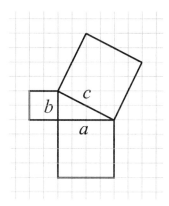

Then the area of the square built on side a will be $a \times a = a^2$, and on sides b and c will be $b \times b = b^2$ and $c \times c = c^2$. So, the theorem can be written as $c^2 = a^2 + b^2$. Surprisingly, the children did not have any problem with the letter notation used in this context.

Teacher ▶ In general the Pythagorean theorem depends on Euclid's fifth postulate. For example, it does not work in non-euclidean geometries. However, since all our squares and triangles have their corners on the grid, we do not need to use this postulate explicitly.

In the previous section we completed the proof of the Pythagorean theorem. Now is the right time to discuss what the word *"proof"* means; we avoided it for so long.

In a court of law if a person is suspected of committing a crime, a prosecutor must prove it beyond a reasonable doubt. In math "beyond a reasonable doubt" is not enough. A proof must withstand any possible attack — it should be watertight.

So, a proof is not just a plausible argument. It's a sequence of statements leading to a certain conclusion, where each claim follows from the previous ones and, possibly, from some previously established facts. Everyone who follows a proof ends up convinced that the conclusion is true.

If a proof is complete, its truth is established forever. Thousands of years have passed since Pythagoras's times, empires fell, new languages evolved, yet his theorem is still true, and now there are many different ways to prove it.

This is how it is supposed to be. In reality, there are famous examples of important "proofs", which were found faulty, and even famous "theorems" were found to be wrong after decades of being considered watertight.

Wouldn't it be interesting if musicians shared the process of creating beautiful melodies with all listeners? If everybody with a good ear could improve a melody and make it more harmonious? It sounds preposterous but this is exactly what happens in mathematics. Any listener or reader of a proof shares with the author the burden of finding errors.

Proofs are contagious. If your proof is complete, then a person who reads it is able to share it with others.

To figure out a proof one has to organize one's ideas, pay attention to details, and search for possible flaws. This process frequently leads to unforeseen insights. Also, people sometimes return to unfinished proofs later, after learning new approaches that enable them to make final steps and close the last gaps in a proof.

Teacher Since the children will study the Pythagorean theorem at school we will solve only a few problems using it.

Problem 5.24. Finding a Leg of a Right Triangle. The length of a hypotenuse of a right triangle is 25 and that of one of its legs is 24. Find the length of the other leg.

Teacher For younger students, who are not comfortable with multiplication, this problem should be simplified. For example, the hypotenuse could be 5 or 13, and the leg could be 4 or 12.

The students easily determined the areas of the squares built on the hypotenuse, $25^2 = 25 \times 25 = 625$, and on the given leg, $24^2 = 24 \times 24 = 576$. However, many kids stumbled on finding the area of the third square. Hint: "$24^2 + ?^2 = 25^2$." Finally, the children explained that by the Pythagorean theorem the third square has the area $625 - 576 = 49$. Hence, the second leg must be 7 since $49 = 7 \times 7 = 7^2$. ∎

Problem 5.25. The Longest Side in a Right Triangle. Which of the three sides in a right triangle is the longest?

Teacher This problem is usually solved without the Pythagorean theorem, but our students do not know geometry well enough for that.

The children immediately answered, "The hypotenuse is the longest." However, only some of them were able to defend their claim without a hint: "Draw squares on all sides of the triangle." The area of the square built on the hypotenuse equals the sum of the areas of two squares built on the legs, so it must be the largest. This means that the hypotenuse is the longest side. ∎

Problem 5.26. Compare Segments. Which of the two line segments in picture A below is longer, the red or the black one?

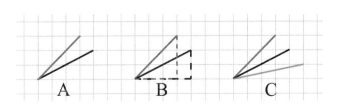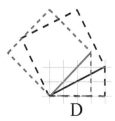

Teacher Some of our younger students make mistakes copying lines and segments into their notebooks. We advise them to draw a right triangle with the desired segment as a hypotenuse (see picture B above). Counting tiles in the legs helps to correctly draw the hypotenuse.

A number of children solved this problem incorrectly. Most of them observed that the red segment is the hypotenuse of the right triangle with legs 3 and 3, and the black segment is the hypotenuse of the right triangle with legs 4 and 2 (picture B). They concluded that since $3 + 3 = 4 + 2$ the segments are equal. To rebuff this claim we drew the third blue segment (picture C), the hypotenuse of the triangle with legs 5 and 1, which according to their reasoning should be as long as the other two segments. However, it is clearly the longest.

Hint: "Despite getting the wrong answer, the triangles you drew are very helpful." After this hint almost everybody found the solution but a few kids still needed another hint: "Imagine tilted squares with the given segments as sides." The kids drew the squares shown in picture D. They argued that according to the Pythagorean theorem the area of the red square is $3^2 + 3^2 = 9 + 9 = 18$ and the area of the black square is $2^2 + 4^2 = 4 + 16 = 20$. Since the black square has a bigger area, the black segment is longer. Although we cannot compute the lengths of the segments, we still can compare their lengths! ∎

Teacher We intentionally removed the grid from picture D above since drawing the squares correctly is not important for this problem and we did not want the kids to waste any time. In this problem the students implicitly used the fact that the square with the longer side has larger area.

Problem 5.27. Three Squares.

- Ann drew a square with the segment shown below as its side. Draw Ann's square. What is its area?
- Bob drew a square with the diagonal of Ann's square as its side. What is the area of Bob's square? Draw Bob's square.
- Carl drew a square with corners on the grid and with an area twice the area of Bob's square. Draw Carl's square.

The most popular way to draw Ann's square involved drawing the right triangle with the given segment as a hypotenuse and copying it three times as shown in the right picture below. The area of Ann's square was found by subtracting the areas of four yellow triangles from the area of the large framing square.

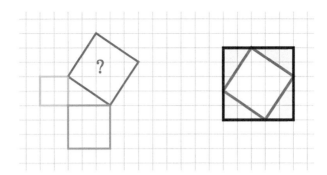

A couple of students started by computing the area of Ann's square using the Pythagorean theorem. They drew the green and blue squares shown above on the left and found the area of Ann's square as the sum of their areas: $2^2 + 3^2 = 13$. These students drew the red square using the method described above.

Bob's square was drawn using the same method as Ann's square:

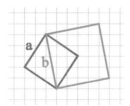

A couple of students noticed that the picture above looks like the picture from Problem 5.4 "Goat". In that problem we discovered that the area of a square built on the diagonal of another square is twice the area of the original square, and so the area of Bob's square is twice the area of Ann's square and is equal to $13 \times 2 = 26$.

Unfortunately, a lot of the kids did not notice the connection with the problem "Goat", and calculated the area of Bob's square using the Pythagorean theorem: $1^2 + 5^2 = 26$. We gave those children a hint: "You just found that the area of Bob's square is twice the area of Ann's square. Is it a coincidence?"

As the children recalled what was done in the beginning of this chapter, some realized that the easiest explanation can be obtained by folding the red square along its blue diagonal. The resulting triangle can also be obtained by folding the blue square along its diagonals into four layers. Hence the area of the blue square is twice the area of the red one.

Now everybody drew Carl's square on the diagonal of Bob's square (see the green square below), and explained that its area is twice the area of Bob's square, and is $26 \times 2 = 52$.

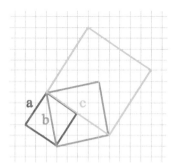

Area of a Parallelogram and Area of a Triangle

Teacher Children study the formulas discussed in this section in school. However, most of them do not understand why those formulas work. While we try to avoid the topics discussed in school at the math circle, we make an exception in this case.

Problem 5.28. Area of a Parallelogram. Which of the two parallelograms below has a larger area?

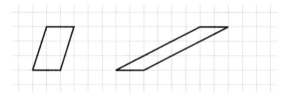

Right away several kids shouted that the area of the left parallelogram is larger, a few others thought that the right one is larger, while the rest of the class insisted that the parallelograms have the same area.

We drew a stack of cards on the board as shown on the left picture below. Then we "tilted" it to the right imagining that the cards stick to each other and to the table so that the stack does not fall. We asked the students to compare the areas of the stacks shown in the picture.

The children replied that since the number of cards and their thickness do not change when the stack is tilted, the area does not change too.

Several kids noticed that the parallelograms from the problem statement and the tilted card stacks are the same except for the "stairs" in the stacks. If the cards were really thin, these "stairs" would be practically invisible. This suggests that the areas of the two original parallelograms are equal to each other and to the area of a rectangle with the same bottom side and the same height. Unfortunately, this explanation is incomplete since we cannot ignore the "stairs".

A couple of students solved the problem by calculating the area of a parallelogram as the product of its base and height, but none were able to explain why this formula works.

Other children found the area of the left parallelogram by cutting a triangular piece along the red line (below in the middle) and moving this triangle to the right, forming a rectangle:

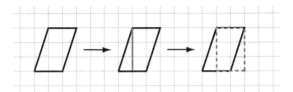

This method, however, doesn't work for the second parallelogram since there is no easy way to cut that parallelogram and rearrange the pieces into a rectangle with sides on the grid.

Hint: "Draw a framing rectangle for each parallelogram." After drawing them (see the top pictures below), the children quickly discovered that the area of each parallelogram is equal to the area of the framing rectangle minus the areas of two yellow right triangles and found that the areas of the parallelograms are equal. Although the children solved this problem, we wanted to take them further to find a general method. We recalled "the universal law of free space" (page 117) and asked, "If each framing rectangle is a room, what plays the role of the tables, and what plays the role of the free space?" The whole class answered immediately, "The yellow triangles are the tables, and the parallelograms are the free space." "Will rearranging the tables help us calculate the area of the free space?" Now almost everybody came up with the new room setup shown on the bottom. The free space became a rectangle.

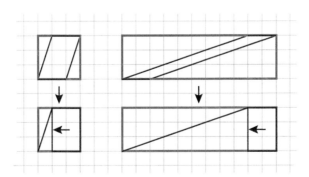

The students concluded that the areas of the top parallelograms are the same as the areas of the bottom rectangles. These rectangles have the same bottom sides (*bases*) and the same *heights* as the parallelograms. So, the area of a parallelogram is equal to the area of a rectangle with the same base and height or "base" × "height". ■

For each triangle on the picture below, the green line connects a corner (vertex) of a triangle with the red line and forms a right angle with the red line. The side of the triangle on this red line is called the *base* and the green segment is called the *height* (or *altitude*) of a triangle.

Problem 5.29. Area of Acute and Obtuse Triangles. For each of the two triangles below draw a parallelogram with the area twice as large and with corners on the grid. Each triangle should be a part of the parallelogram. How does it help to compute the areas of the triangles?

Many students needed a hint: "Near the original triangle draw its copy rotated upside-down." The kids drew the picture:

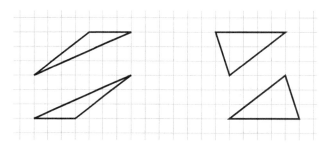

Different children found one of the three possible solutions for each triangle:

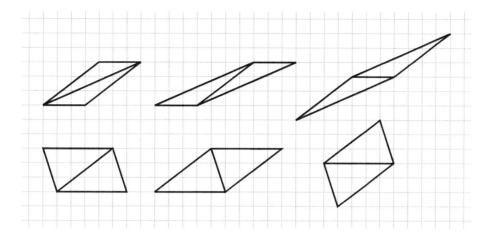

Out of these three solutions we need only the first or the second one since the parallelogram's base and height follow the grid lines only in these cases.

The area of each of the obtained parallelograms is twice as large as the corresponding triangle. Moreover, the first and the second parallelograms have the same base and height. Since the area of a parallelogram is "base" × "height", the area of each triangle is half of "base" × "height". ■

In the last two problems we obtained very interesting results:

- The area of a parallelogram is equal to the area of the rectangle with the same base and height.
- It does not matter whether a triangle is right, acute, or obtuse, its area is equal to half of its base × height.

For the kids who did not know the latter result before, it came as a great surprise.

Pick's Formula

Teacher ▷ We had no expectations that students would solve the following problem. Our main goal was to show the class how non-trivial Picks' formula is.

In the following discussion we refer to corners of the grid squares as "grid points".

Problem 5.30. Area and Grid Points. Patrick thinks that he can find the area of a shape with corners on the grid if you tell him the number of grid points inside and on the borders of the shape. Try to come up with a recipe which will work for the following shapes:

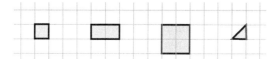

Looking at a 1×1 square the students immediately proposed to mark the corners in red and count each red point as 1/4. After studying a 2×1 rectangle the kids decided to mark the remaining grid points on the sides yellow and count each of them as 1/2. The next shape, a 2×2 square, led to yet another suggestion, "Mark inside grid points green and count each of them as 1." Finally, the last shape on the right demonstrated that the previous suggestions do not work: its true area is $\frac{1}{2}$, while the proposed formula gives $\frac{3}{4}$!

So, if there is a recipe that works, it is not that easy to find by considering these simple examples. Instead of continuing the search, we disclosed the answer in the following problem. ■

Problem 5.31. Patrick's Formula. Patrick thinks that he can find the area of a shape in the following way:

- He marks in red all the grid points on the sides.
- He marks in green all the grid points inside the shape.
- He counts the number of green points and adds half of the number of red points.
- Then he subtracts 1, and gets the area.

Will Patrick's recipe work?

First, we decided to check if Patrick's recipe works for the shapes in the previous problem. It worked for all four of them, so it appeared that the recipe works. However, the examples from the previous problem were quite simple. Let us check Patrick's formula using more complex shapes, for example, the shapes shown below:

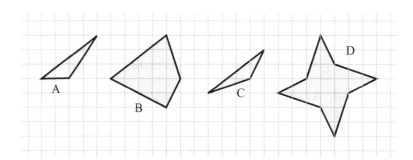

The children used many methods to find the areas of the shapes above; here we list only the most common ones.

For the triangle A the area may be calculated as base $\times$ height $\div 2$: $(2 \times 3) \div 2 = 3$.

For the quadrilateral B the easiest approach was to split it into two triangles using a vertical or horizontal line. For instance, using the horizontal line one gets two triangles of areas $(5 \times 3) \div 2 = 7\frac{1}{2}$ and $(5 \times 2) \div 2 = 5$. So, the shape has area $12\frac{1}{2}$.

For the triangle C the students first found the area of the large multi-colored right triangle (see below). Then, they subtracted from it the areas of yellow and green triangles, as well as the area of a small pink square: $(4 \times 3) \div 2 - (3 \times 1) \div 2 - (2 \times 1) \div 2 - 1 = 6 - 1\frac{1}{2} - 1 - 1 = 2\frac{1}{2}$.

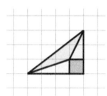

Teacher We never write such long expressions in our classes. Instead we break the calculations into parts. Moreover, many of our students do not know the order of operations and/or parentheses. This forces us to use expressions like half of 5×3.

Finding the area of the star D presented no conceptual difficulties. This shape can be split into four green triangles each of area $(2 \times 1) \div 2$, four blue triangles each of area $(2 \times 1) \div 2$, and the yellow cross of area 5. Hence, the total area is $6 + 4 + 5 = 15$.

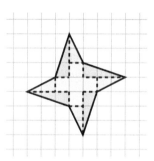

Then the children colored the grid points according to Patrick's recipe:

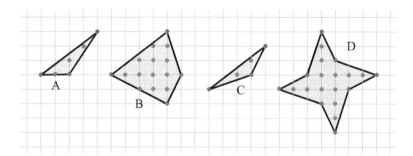

The students calculated the areas of all shapes using Patrick's formula and put their results into the table:

	A	B	C	D
Area	3	$12\frac{1}{2}$	$2\frac{1}{2}$	15
Green	2	11	2	12
Red	4	5	3	8
Patrick	$2+4\div2-1$	$11+5\div2-1$	$2+3\div2-1$	$12+8\div2-1$
Result	3	$12\frac{1}{2}$	$2\frac{1}{2}$	15

The kids concluded that for all the shapes we studied so far Patrick's formula gave the correct result. ■

Patrick's recipe written as Area $=$ Green $+\frac{1}{2}$Red -1 is called *Pick's formula*.

Georg Alexander Pick discovered this formula and proved it in 1899. This is a very recent discovery compared to all other mathematics children study in elementary or middle school.

The children were convinced that Pick's formula always works. To prove them wrong we had to look at some other shapes.

Problem 5.32. Pick's Formula Doesn't Always Work. Come up with shapes for which Pick's formula gives the wrong answer.

In some classes the picture with the shapes below were given to the kids (without marked points). In other classes the children were able to come up with such examples on their own after we gave them a hint: "The shapes we considered before are not weird, one needs a weird enough shape."

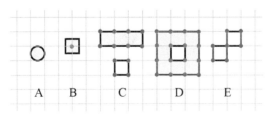

After marking the points the children quickly completed the calculations presented below:

	A	B	C	D	E
Area	<1	1	4	8	2
Green	0	1	0	0	0
Red	0	0	12	16	7
Pick	$0+0\div2-1$	$1+0\div2-1$	$0+12\div2-1$	$0+16\div2-1$	$0+7\div2-1$
Result	-1	0	5	7	$2\frac{1}{2}$

The children were particularly excited by the results they got for shapes A and B. A few kids even noticed that making circle A smaller would make its area smaller, but it does not change the number of colored points. Then other kids made similar observation for square B: increasing it a little bit does not change its area according to Pick's formula.

The kids argued whether picture C presents one or two shapes. We drew letter "i" on the board and asked, "Is it one shape or two? Since we had no prior agreement on what makes a shape, we are free to consider it as one shape." ■

We asked the kids, "Based on the results of this problem try to come up with the list of conditions under which Pick's formula works." Eventually, with our help the class arrived at the following list. The shape must:

- have straight edges;
- have corners on the grid;
- there should be precisely two edges meeting at every corner;
- consist of only one piece;
- have no holes.

The students felt quite disappointed that Pick's formula does not work in so many cases. It turns out that it may be fixed for shapes consisting of multiple pieces and/or having holes.

Teacher ▷ For the next two problems we drew the shapes and the children colored the grid points red and green themselves.

Problem 5.33. Pick's Formula: Shapes with Multiple Pieces. Compare the results obtained using Pick's formula with the actual areas for the shapes below. Can you suggest a correction to Pick's formula?

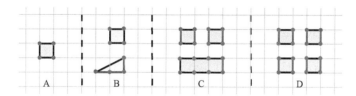

In a couple of minutes the class found the actual areas and the results of Pick's formula. We suggested recording the answers in the table:

Number of pieces	Pick	Actual area
1	1	1
2	3	2
3	7	5
4	7	4

Once the results were recorded systematically, the students had no difficulties modifying Pick's formula as Area = Green + Red ÷ 2 − Pieces. This formula seems to work for shapes consisting of multiple pieces. ■

Problem 5.34. Pick's Formula: Shapes with Holes. Compare the results obtained by Pick's formula with the actual areas for the following shapes. Can you suggest another correction to Pick's formula?

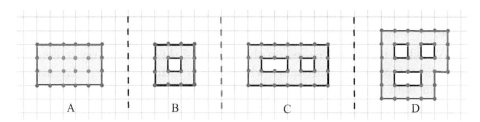

Again the children quickly computed all areas in two ways and recorded their results in the following table:

Number of holes	Pick	Actual area
0	15	15
1	7	8
2	13	15
3	16	19

This time Pick's formula should be modified as Area = Green + Red ÷ 2 − 1 + Holes. ■

As we just found Area = Green + Red ÷ 2 − Pieces works if we have no holes, and Area = Green+Red÷2−1+Holes works if we have only one piece. We asked the class if they can propose an expression which would work in both these cases. They arrived at Area = Green + Red ÷ 2 − Pieces + Holes, which turns out to be the correct expression.

Since we have not considered any examples of shapes that have both several pieces and holes, the last formula is just a hypothesis. Actually, all formulas in this section are still hypotheses for us. We just looked at a few examples, and testing a few cases is not a proof.

A number of students were curious about why Pick's formula works. However, the proof of Pick's formula is beyond the abilities of our students. They might return to it in a few years. For now we wanted to introduce this formula to the kids, let them discover how it works, and what its limitations are.

Chapter 6

Selected Warmup and Challenging Problems

The first few problems in this chapter are related to the five main themes presented in this book (Chapters 1–5). Most of these problems should be given before the corresponding topic is discussed, while several are follow-up questions (see Notes to the Teacher). The rest of the problems are included for the convenience of an instructor, allowing one to use a single source for lesson preparations. Some of these problems are original problems, but the vast majority are well known.

Teacher ▸ The following problem may be given at the beginning of Chapter 1, "Numbers as Geometric Shapes", to facilitate the discussion of differences: what it means to subtract pictures.

Problem 6.1. Find the sum or the difference for pictures inside the red squares.

The children received handouts (see the left-hand sides of the equalities in the pictures below). Most students had no doubts about how to draw the sums: the pictures should be overlaid. Everybody decided not to draw a segment twice if it is present on both pictures. There were only a few errors in copying the segments.

Subtracting pictures turned out to be a little harder. After a short discussion the students decided that subtraction should mean erasing those parts of the first picture that were present in the second. Then, everybody got the correct answers:

Several kids asked what would happen if the subtrahend has lines not present in the minuend. For example, if a square with a single line is subtracted from the empty square. Some students thought such an operation is not allowed; others argued that since we defined subtracting pictures as erasing, this operation should be allowed but nothing would happen. We commented that such cases are a matter of agreement, and agreed with the interpretation offered by the latter group.   ■

Teacher The next problem is about L-shapes introduced in Chapter 1, "Numbers as Geometric Shapes". It can be given soon after L-shapes are studied.

Problem 6.2. Using 3-tile L-shapes, ⌐, tile the following shapes.

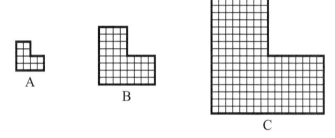

The tiling of shape A was found by trial and error very quickly:

For shape B the students came up with a couple of different solutions. Most did it by trial and error. Only a few kids noticed that the picture above also shows how to tile shape B with shape A. We wanted everyone to see this approach, and gave the class a hint: "Tiling shape A helps tiling shape B." Now the children tiled shape B with 3-tile L-shapes in no time:

After discussing how to tile shape B the majority of the children found how to tile shape C almost immediately. They proposed to tile it with shape B, correctly claiming that it is the same problem once again.   ■

Teacher The following problem is about grouping numbers. It can be given prior to the discussion of "Gauss's method" for adding numbers in Chapter 1, "Numbers as Geometric Shapes".

Problem 6.3. Sam found seven different stones. The stones weigh:
(1) (harder version) 19, 21, 23, 38, 40, 42, and 61 pounds;
(2) (easier version) 1, 2, 3, 4, 5, 6, and 7 pounds.

Sam put his stones into four different bags in such a way that the weights of all bags are the same. How did he do it?

(1) One of the ways the children solved the problem was to determine the weight of each bag first. They added the weights of all stones, divided the sum by 4, and found that each bag should weigh 61 lbs. Grouping lighter stones with heavier stones and leaving the heaviest stone by itself they got 4 groups: 61, 19 and 42, 21 and 40, 23 and 38.

(2) While several students who were given the easier version, solved the problem as outlined above, others did it without finding the weight of each bag. Instead, they arranged the stones by trial and error. Everyone got the bags with weights: 7, 1 and 6, 2 and 5, 3 and 4. ■

Teacher ▶ In the next few problems the children have to compute the number of items in a range. In these situations students often make the so-called "off by 1" error, when "the obvious answer" is one more or one less than the correct answer. These problems should be given before covering Chapter 2, "Combinatorics".

Problem 6.4. The doctor gave Ann eight pills and told her to take one pill every half an hour. How long will it take Ann to finish the pills after she started taking them?

Several students immediately gave the wrong answer: $8 \times \frac{1}{2} = 4$ hours. They did not realize that they need to compute the total time in all the gaps between the pills. A few children drew eight pills, and counted seven gaps between them. Others got the same number of gaps without drawing a picture. Since each gap is half an hour, the kids added seven halves and got the answer $3\frac{1}{2}$ hours.   ■

Problem 6.5. How many two-digit numbers are there? Three-digit numbers?

Before the children started solving the problem we asked, "What are the smallest and the largest two- and three-digit numbers?" The kids replied, "They are 10 and 99, and 100 and 999."

Several students thought that for two-digit numbers the right answer is: $99 - 10 = 89$. Others decided that the answer is 90 because there are 99 numbers from 1 through 99, but nine of them, 1 through 9, are one-digit numbers and should not be counted. We asked the children which of the answers is correct. After some pondering the first group realized, "We did not count 10!" They corrected themselves: $99 - 10 + 1 = 90$.

The class used the same two approaches to compute all 3-digit numbers. There are 999 numbers from 1 to 999. Crossing out one- and two-digit numbers, 1 through 99, the kids found the answer $999 - 99 = 900$ three-digit numbers.   ■

Problem 6.6. A beaver Brian cuts logs into smaller pieces with his teeth. He always cuts across a log and only one log at a time.

  (1) Brian took one log and made 10 cuts. How many pieces did he get?

  (2) Brian took three logs and made 10 cuts. How many pieces could he get?

  (3) Brian made 10 cuts and got 16 pieces. How many logs did he start with?

(1) Everyone promptly drew a log and marked 10 cuts on it getting 11 pieces. We asked the children to explain what happens to the log step by step. When the beaver cuts a log once, he gets 2 pieces. Then Brian cuts the log the second time and gets 3 pieces, and so on. Recording these results in a table we got:

Number of cuts	0	1	2	...	10
Number of pieces	1	2	3	...	11

    The children observed that each cut creates an additional piece and, therefore, the number of pieces is always one more than the number of cuts. The beaver started with one piece since one log is a piece too. Thus, "number of pieces" = "number of cuts" + 1.

(2) A number of children proposed to put three original logs next to each other forming one log that was already cut twice. This means that cutting three logs 10 times is the same as cutting one log 12 times. According to the first part of the problem, it results in $12 + 1 = 13$ pieces.

    The majority of the students found the correct answer 13 by drawing a picture for a specific way of cutting logs. However, many of them couldn't explain why the answer doesn't depend on the way Brian cuts the logs. Hint: "What happens when the beaver makes a single cut?" The kids explained that Brian started with three pieces and each cut he makes creates an additional piece. 10 cuts adds 10 pieces. So, it doesn't matter how the beaver cuts his logs; he always ends up with $3 + 10 = 13$ pieces.

    In general, since every cut adds a new piece to the existing pieces (logs) Brian already has, we get the formula for any number of logs and cuts: "number of pieces = number of cuts + number of logs".

(3) Once everybody realized that according to the above formula "number of logs = number of pieces−number of cuts", the kids determined that initially Brian had $16 - 10 = 6$ logs. ∎

Problem 6.7. Two players take turns breaking a chocolate bar: a player can break only one piece at a time and only along score lines. The last person who is able to break a piece into smaller ones wins the game. Who wins if:

(1) The bar consists of 15 squares; the score lines divide it into five rows and three columns?

(2) The bar consists of 30 squares; the score lines divide it into five rows and six columns?

To clarify the rules of the game we drew the first chocolate bar on the board and invited two kids to play the game in front of the whole class.

Even though this problem is very similar to the previous problem, only one or two students solved it right away. So we asked the class to split into pairs and play the game a few times using a drawing of a 5×3 chocolate bar.

Most of the children observed that for a 5×3 bar the second player always wins. However, they were not sure whether this outcome was independent of the way the bar was broken. Hint: "Look at the end pictures for all the different rounds you played. Do you see any similarities between them?" The children noticed that there were always 15 single squares left. In a few minutes many students realized that every time the bar is broken the number of pieces increases by one. Hence, a bar with 15 squares can be broken 14 times and the second player always wins. Similarly, the bar with 30 squares can be broken 29 times and the first player always wins. ■

Problem 6.8. Tom was reading a book and discovered that some of the pages were missing. Page 103 followed right after page 46. How many pages were missing from the book?

Many children immediately decided that the answer is $103 - 46 = 57$. To show them their mistake we asked, "How many pages are missing if page 47 follows page 46?" Returning to Tom's book, the children realized that neither page 46 nor page 103 are missing. The difference $103 - 46$ counts pages 46 through 103 not including 46 but including 103. Hence, the answer is $103 - 46 - 1 = 56$. ■

Problem 6.9. It takes 12 seconds for the elevator to get from the 1st floor to the 3rd floor. How long does it take the elevator to get from the 1st floor to the 6th floor?

As soon as the children read the problem they shouted, "24 since 6 is twice bigger than 3." This seemingly obvious answer is incorrect. To solve the problem the majority of the children had to draw a 6-story house. The drawing helped the kids to see that the elevator passes only two gaps between the floors when it goes from the 1st to the 3rd floor. So it takes the elevator $12 \div 2 = 6$ seconds to pass a floor. The elevator passes five gaps between the floors to get from the 1st to the 6th floor. Thus, the answer is $5 \times 6 = 30$ seconds. ■

Teacher ➤ The following problem should be given before one teaches Chapter 3, "Fibonacci Numbers".

Problem 6.10. Guess the next two numbers for the following sequences:

(1) $1, 3, 5, 7, \ldots$.

(2) $2, 5, 8, 11, 14, \ldots$.

(3) $2, 3, 5, 8, 12, 17, \ldots$.

(4) $1, 2, 4, 8, \ldots$.

(5) $1, 4, 9, 16, \ldots$.

(6) $2, 4, 6, 10, 16, 26, \ldots$.

First, we pointed out that in this problem we assume that the numbers in each sequence are obtained according to some rule. Otherwise, this kind of question makes no sense. This point is well illustrated by sequence 7, 11, 13, 15, 19, 22. The "correct" next two items are 28 and 48 since this sequence represents the prices of ice cream in Moscow in the 1970s.

The children had no difficulties with the first three sequences. Only a couple of students struggled with sequences (4) and (5). Sequence (6) turned out to be hard.

(1) $1, 3, 5, 7, \ldots$ is a sequence of odd numbers starting with 1. The next two terms are 9 and 11.

(2) The difference between the two consecutive numbers in this sequence is always 3. So, the next two terms are 17 and 20.

(3) The differences between the consecutive numbers in the sequence 2, 3, 5, 8, 12, 17, ... are 1, 2, 3, 4, 5, ... The next two terms of the latter sequence are 6 and 7, which means that the next two terms of the original sequence are $17 + 6 = 23$ and $23 + 7 = 30$. Some kids noticed that if the sequence were to begin with 1, it would be a sequence of triangular numbers.

(4) Everybody noticed that each new term of this sequence is twice larger than the previous term. Therefore the next two numbers are 16 and 32. Many older students recognized that this sequence contains powers of 2.

(5) Most of the children saw right away that $1, 4, 9, 16$ are consecutive square numbers. The next two square numbers are $5 \times 5 = 25$ and $6 \times 6 = 36$.

(6) A number of students found that the differences between consecutive terms are $2, 2, 4, 6, 10, \ldots$ and got stuck. Hint: "Do you recognize this sequence?" The students replied that starting with the second term this is the same sequence as the given one. So, the next difference should be 16, and the next number should be $26 + 16 = 42$. The difference after that should be 26, and the next number is $42 + 26 = 68$.

A few other kids observed that each term of the given sequence is the sum of two previous terms, and computed the same answers.

We asked the class, "Why do the two computations above give the same result?" Only a couple of kids were able to illustrate the connection. They drew the following picture:

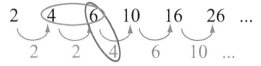

Indeed, if 10 is the sum of 4 and 6 in the blue oval, the difference between 10 and 6 is again 4 (in the red oval). ■

Teacher The next four problems should be given at the beginning of Chapter 4, "Pascal's Triangle".

Problem 6.11. A squirrel mom brought home some nuts, and her kids, Adam, Beth, Carl, Don, and Eva, ate all but one of them. First Adam ate half of all the nuts, then Beth ate half of the remaining nuts, and so on. How many nuts did the mother bring? How many nuts did each kid eat? How many nuts did all the kids eat together? If there were six greedy baby squirrels in the family, how many nuts would they eat all together?

Note that greedy squirrels always eat whole nuts.

Right away the children gave a variety of answers: 12 nuts, 26 nuts, etc. Checking these guesses, we found that all of them were incorrect. For example, if there were 12 nuts at the beginning, Adam would eat 6 nuts, Beth would eat 3, and Carl would have a problem: he cannot divide 3 into two equal whole numbers.

Hint: "Draw the picture while reading the problem." Many kids used a long strip (strip 1 below) to represent all nuts that mom brought. Then strips 2 through 6 show what happened when Adam, then Beth, then all other kids came and ate half of the remaining nuts.

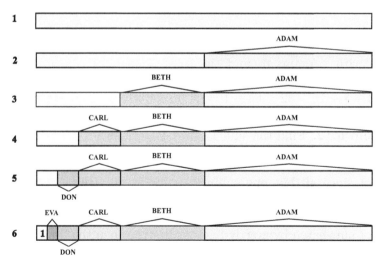

Most of the class finished the problem on their own, but several kids needed another hint: "Go through the problem in the reverse order, from strip 6 to strip 1."

The kids explained that when Eva came, she saw nuts represented by yellow and purple rectangles in strip 6. She ate half of them (the purple rectangle) and left the other half (the yellow rectangle). It means that Eva ate one nut and there were two nuts left after Don (shown as a yellow rectangle in strip 5). Similarly, when Don came, he discovered nuts shown as yellow and gray rectangles in strip 5. He ate half of them (the gray rectangle) and left the other half. This means that he ate two nuts and there were four left after Carl (shown as a yellow rectangle in strip 4). Continuing in the same manner, the children determined that Carl ate four nuts, Beth ate eight nuts and Adam ate 16 nuts. These results are illustrated in the picture below:

Now the class was ready to compute the total number of nuts eaten by the squirrels:

$1 + 2 + 4 + 8 + 16 = 31.$

"Is there a way to find this answer without doing so many additions?" Many children needed a hint to answer this question: "Look at all the numbers in the picture above, both blue and orange." The children explained that the total number of eaten nuts (sum of blue numbers) can be computed as the difference between 32 nuts that mom had at the beginning and 1 nut that was left at the end (difference of two orange numbers). Hence, $1 + 2 + 4 + 8 + 16 = 32 - 1 = 31.$

"What if there were six greedy baby squirrels in the family?" A few children got the answer almost immediately but several had to repeat the entire argument. Eventually, everyone figured out that there were 64 nuts to begin with. Again, to find the total number of consumed nuts, one can subtract the remaining 1 from the initial amount, 64. It means that $1 + 2 + 4 + 8 + 16 + 32 = 64 - 1 = 63$ nuts were eaten by six squirrels. ■

Problem 6.12. Find the sum $1 + 2 + 4 + 8 + 16 + \cdots + 1024$.

At first many kids thought that the sum is 2048. This answer cannot be correct since all but one summands are even! Hint: "Come up with the problem about baby squirrels similar to the previous one that has the desired sum as the answer." The students associated the given sum with the number of nuts eaten by greedy baby squirrels. Then the first baby squirrel ate 1024 nuts. Since he ate half of the nuts on the table, there were 2048 nuts on the table at the beginning. After all the squirrels ate their shares, one nut remained. It means the number of nuts eaten by baby squirrels is $2048 - 1 = 2047.$ ■

Teacher Before stating the next problem we reminded the class about the Ancestry Trees (page 64, Chapter 3, "Fibonacci Numbers").

Here is an example of a human ancestry tree:

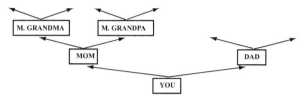

We count ancestors starting with Mom and Dad in the 1st generation. Notice that all human ancestry trees include oneself in the 0th generation.

Problem 6.13.

(1) Draw the human ancestry tree through the 5th generation. How many ancestors are there in generations 1, 2, 3, 4, and 5?

(2) Find how many ancestors there are in the 10th generation without drawing a bigger tree.

(3) How many people are there in the ancestry tree with four generations? nine generations?

(1) The children quickly drew the picture (only a piece is shown below) and computed the results shown in green:

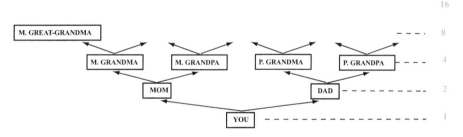

The students explained that the number of ancestors in a given generation is twice bigger than the number of ancestors in the previous generation. Indeed, each person in the previous generation has a mother and a father. For example, each grandparent has two parents and there are $4 + 4 = 2 \times 4 = 8$ great-grandparents.

(2) There are $2 \times 2 \times 2 \times 2 \times 2 \times 2 \times 2 \times 2 \times 2 \times 2 = 2^{10} = 1024$ ancestors in the 10th generation.

(3) To compute the total number of people in the ancestry tree with four generations many children added the green numbers in the picture above: $1 + 2 + 4 + 8 + 16 = 31$. They recalled the previous warmup problem and computed the number of people in the ancestry tree with nine generations: $1 + 2 + 4 + \ldots + 2^9 = 2^{10} - 1 = 1024 - 1 = 1023$. ∎

Teacher ➤ The following problem should precede the "More Triangles in a Square" problem in Chapter 5, "Area".

Problem 6.14. Ann, Bob, and Carl want to make squares for their origami projects.

- Ann plans to check that all the sides of her quadrilateral are of equal length.
- Bob plans to check that two diagonals in his quadrilateral are of equal length.
- Carl plans to cut his quadrilateral into four pieces along the diagonals and check that all four pieces are SAME SHAPE SAME SIZE.

Will their methods work?

A number of students promptly claimed that Ann's method works because in a square all sides are equal. We explained that a valid method must guarantee that any quadrilateral satisfying listed conditions is always a square. For example, if Ann's method works, then all quadrilaterals with four equal sides are squares. Several children immediately drew a rhombus (see picture A below), which is a quadrilateral with four equal sides but not a square. So, Ann's method does not work.

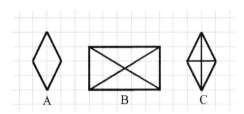

Teacher ➤ At this time we usually discuss with the children that one needs a single counterexample to show that a statement is incorrect.

The majority of the children had no difficulty giving a counterexample for Bob's method. Most of them drew a rectangle (see picture B above). A few kids needed a hint: "Draw two equal segments that would be the diagonals of a quadrilateral, and then draw the quadrilateral itself." A couple of students needed more help and we gave them two sticks of the same length, "Draw different quadrilaterals with these sticks as the diagonals."

Since we didn't erase the counterexamples to Ann's and Bob's methods from the board, the children came up with the counterexample for Carl's method very quickly. They pointed out that a rhombus would work as a counterexample for Carl's method too (picture C above). ∎

Teacher ➤ The next three problems develop further the idea of similar shapes and should be given after the corresponding problems from Chapter 5, "Area".

Problem 6.15. Linda made a model pumpkin out of building blocks (every block is a solid plastic cube). Melissa made another pumpkin using the same design but her building blocks (also solid plastic cubes) were three times higher. How many times heavier is Melissa's model than Linda's model?

A number of children needed a hint: "Imagine that the larger building blocks are made out of the smaller ones." As the kids discovered in Chapter 1, "Numbers as Geometric Shapes", it takes 27 small blocks to make each of the big blocks. Hence, one big block is 27 times heavier than the small block. The students concluded that it does not matter how many blocks were used in the pumpkin design as long as the same number of blocks were used by both girls. Melissa's pumpkin is 27 times heavier than Linda's. ∎

Problem 6.16. Linda and Melissa each got a plastic (solid) pumpkin as a present. They are of the same shape, but Melissa's is three times higher. How many times heavier is Melissa's pumpkin than Linda's pumpkin?

Only a few children noticed that this problem is the same as the previous one. Hint for the rest of the class: "Think of real pumpkins as made out of tiny cubes." Several students thought that 3 is the answer. They had to think for some time and solve the previous problem once again before arriving at the correct answer. Since Melissa's model pumpkin is 27 times heavier, Melissa's real pumpkin is also 27 times heavier. ∎

Problem 6.17. A baby elephant weighs one ton. His mother has the same shape as her baby but she is four times taller. What is her weight?

A number of kids immediately stated that the shape of an elephant doesn't matter, drew a baby elephant as a little cube, and gave the correct answer 64.

At the same time surprisingly many students struggled with this problem and gave 4 or 16 as their first answer. They had to think of modeled elephants (most imagined elephants made of Legos) and go through all arguments made in the previous two problems. Eventually, they figured out that since the mother is four times higher, wider, and deeper, she is $4 \times 4 \times 4 = 64$ times heavier than the baby. ∎

Teacher ▸ The next three problems are intended for the first or the last lessons of the year. They should be read to the children, not written down.

Problem 6.18. I have two US coins that are worth 30 cents. One of the coins is not a nickel. What are the two coins?

The majority of the children immediately decided that this problem has no solution. We had to repeat the problem statement a few times before almost everybody perceived that when I have a nickel and a quarter, one of the coins is not a nickel. ∎

Problem 6.19. There were seven candles lit on a birthday cake. Trevor tried to blow them out but managed to do it with only two candles. How many candles were left on the cake?

Many children shouted "five" as soon as they heard the problem. After we told them that five is the wrong answer, the children quickly figured out two correct solutions.

The majority concluded that there were still seven candles on the cake: five burning and two not. A few students said that if one waits for a few minutes, there would be only two candles on the cake since five burning candles would melt down.   ∎

Problem 6.20. How many ends do three hotdogs have? How many ends do four and an half hotdogs have?

Quite a few of our younger students got this problem wrong: their answers were 6 and 9. They were very happy and giggled as they realized that even a half of a hotdog has two ends. The correct answers are 6 and 10.   ∎

Teacher ▷ In our experience children enjoy solving the next few problems. We give them as warmups when the main topic is challenging.

Problem 6.21. Place three chairs in a square room, so that there is a chair by each wall.

The majority of the kids solved the problem very quickly. Put one chair in the corner as shown below. Then it stands by two walls. Place the two remaining chairs by the two remaining walls, one chair per wall:

∎

Problem 6.22. Place four chairs in a square room, so that there are two chairs by each wall.

This problem was solved in no time. Put all four chairs into the corners as shown below. Then each chair is next to two walls, so there are two chairs by each wall.

∎

Problem 6.23. Place 10 chairs in a square room, so that there are three chairs by each wall.

The children quickly found two different answers to the problem:

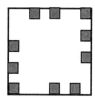

Problem 6.24. Turn the arrangement of coins on the left into the arrangement on the right by moving only three coins.

For this problem we gave the children coins and quite soon most of them found the solution. Hint for the rest: "How many coins were not moved? Find these coins." There should be $10 - 3 = 7$ coins that are arranged in the same way both on the left and on the right. Once the kids found this seven coin arrangement (see below), they quickly finished the problem.

In the picture below red, blue, and green colors denote the coins before and after they were moved:

Problem 6.25. Sam has three toys: a car, an airplane, and a ball. They are stored in three boxes, round, square, and triangular, with one toy per box.

- Neither the ball nor the airplane is in the round box.
- The ball is not in a square box.

Which toy is in which box?

The class easily solved this problem. Since neither the ball nor the airplane are in the round box, it contains the car. Since the square box cannot contain the ball or the car, it has the airplane. It leaves the ball for the triangular box. To find the solution many students drew the table:

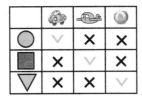

Problem 6.26. There are four houses numbered 1, 2, 3, and 4 on Baker Street. Ted, Alice, Sam, and Emma live in those houses, one in each house. Use the following clues to find out who lives in which house.

- The number of Ted's house is even.
- The number of Sam's house is odd.
- The number of Alice's house is greater than the number of Ted's house.
- The number of Emma's house is less than the number of Sam's house.

Several children drew a table to find the solution but the students who reasoned through the problem without the table found the answer even faster. These kids explained that Ted lives in house 2 or 4 since his number is even. Since Alice's number is greater than Ted's, Ted's number cannot be 4, it is 2. Sam's house is odd: 1 or 3. Emma's number is less than Sam's, which means Sam's is not 1; it is 3. Alice's number is greater than Ted's but not 3. It must be 4. Emma's number has to be 1.   ∎

Problem 6.27. Witchy, Ghosty, Slimy, and Stinky are flying on their brooms one after another in a single file. Slimy is flying next to Witchy but not next to Stinky. Ghosty is not next to Stinky. Who is flying next to Ghosty?

The children reasoned that since neither Slimy nor Ghosty are next to Stinky, Stinky has to be at one end of the line next to Witchy. Slimy, who is flying next to Witchy, follows. Ghosty is at the other end of the line. Hence, the answer is Witchy.   ∎

Problem 6.28. Tom has dogs, cats, and parrots. How many pets does Tom have if:

- all of them but two are dogs;
- all of them but two are cats;
- all of them but two are parrots?

The majority of the children solved this problem by trial and error. Almost everyone started by guessing that there are six animals, two of each kind. This answer is incorrect since in such a case there are four animals that are not dogs, etc. The kids concluded that there should be fewer animals.

It led them to the correct answer, "Tom has only three animals, one of each kind."

A number of children got the same answer differently. They reasoned that since only two animals are not dogs, Tom has either one cat and one parrot, or two cats and no parrots, or two parrots and no cats. The last two cases are impossible. Indeed, if, for example, Tom had two cats, he could not have dogs since only two animals are not parrots. However, if all his animals were cats, the condition that two animals are not cats is violated. Hence, Tom must have one cat and one parrot. Since two animals are not cats, Tom also has one dog.   ■

Problem 6.29. Three friends, Tom, Rick, and Dan, played soccer in the yard. One of the boys accidentally broke a window. When Dan's mom came, Dan said, "Rick broke the window." Tom said, "I did not break the window." Only one of the boys told the truth. Who broke the window?

A few children started by considering possibilities: Tom broke the window, or Rick broke it, or Dan broke it. However, thinking about who lies and who tells the truth leads to the answer much quicker. So, if Tom lies, then he broke the window, and hence Dan lies too. Thus, Tom tells the truth, but Dan lies, and it was he, not Rick, who broke the window.   ■

Problem 6.30. I had three boxes with plants, which were labeled "Cukes", "Flowers", and "Daisies". I planted cucumbers, daisies, and tulips in these boxes. However, I managed to plant them so that all markings were wrong. What was planted in the box labeled "Daisies"?

Only a couple of children solved this problem using a table. The majority of the students quickly figured out that only cucumbers could be planted in the box labeled "Flowers" since both daisies and tulips are flowers. Daisies cannot be in the box labeled "Daisies", so there are tulips in that box.   ■

Problem 6.31. The parliament of Nowhere Land has 100 members. They are so corrupt that in any group of three members there is at least one crook. What is the largest number of honest people that can be in this parliament?

Several students found the answer to the problem very fast and started laughing. In a couple of minutes the entire class became very animated; the children were raising their hands and wanted to explain their solution, "If there are three or more honest people in the parliament, they can form a group of three with no crooks. So, there are at most two honest people in the parliament."   ■

Problem 6.32. The Davidsons have five sons. Each son has exactly one sister. How many children are there in the family?

Many students thought that there were 10 children in the family. We told these students to make a schematic drawing of all children in the family. Here is what they drew:

We asked, "How many sisters does each boy in the picture have?" Looking at the picture most of the students saw at once that each boy has five sisters. However, a couple of children still thought there was only one sister for each brother, the one drawn directly below. We asked these children, "How many brothers does each boy in the picture have?" Then all students figured out that there are six children in the family since the only girl is everybody's sister. ■

Problem 6.33. Ben has as many brothers as he has sisters. His sister Liz has twice as many brothers as she has sisters. How many boys and girls are in that family?

The majority of the students solved this problem by trial and error. First, they figured out that the family should have at least two boys and two girls (otherwise no comparisons are possible) and drew two boys and two girls as stick figures. This combination did not work since Ben should have as many brothers as sisters. So the third boy was added to the family. However, in this case Liz has three times more brothers than sisters. If the fourth boy is added to the family, the third girl should be added as well since Ben should have as many brothers as sisters. Now Liz has two sisters and four brothers, which is exactly as it should be. The family has three girls and four boys.

A couple of kids solved this problem using bars to represent children in the family and quickly found the answer without trial and error:

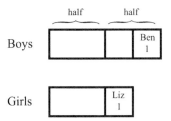

Problem 6.34. Kate has five chain segments. Each segment is three rings long. Kate wants to make a single chain out of these segments. What is the smallest number of rings she needs to break and reseal?

The children answered right away, "It is four because five chain segments should be connected in four places to make a single chain." They were surprised when we claimed that Kate could cut fewer rings. Many of the students asked for strips of paper and tape. They made model chain pieces and tried cutting them in different places. They soon discovered that if all three rings of one of the segments were open, only four remaining chain segments need to be connected. This can be achieved using three already open rings as shown in the picture below.

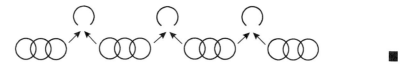

■

Problem 6.35. How many two-digit numbers such that the sum of their digits is 13 are there?

A two-digit number with the sum of digits 13 cannot begin with digits 1, 2, or 3 since the largest possible second digit is 9. It means that 49 is the smallest such number. Also, once the first digit is chosen, the second is already defined as 13 minus the first digit. Hence there are 6 such numbers: 49, 58, 67, 76, 85, 94. Only a couple of students made mistakes in this problem because they listed the numbers without a system.   ■

Teacher▶ The next four problems are easily solved by older children, but are surprisingly difficult for many younger ones.

Problem 6.36. Dana is one year younger than Maya. In two years the sum of their ages will be 15. How old are the girls now?

Hint for the kids who got stuck: "What would be the differences in girls' ages in two years?" Once the students understood that Dana is always going to be one year younger than Maya, they were able to compute the girls' ages in two years. If both girls were as old as Dana, the sum of their ages would be $15 - 1 = 14$ and each of them would be $14 \div 2 = 7$. So, in two years Dana will be 7 and Maya will be 8. It means that now Dana is 5 and Maya is 6.

A number of kids solved this problem differently. They realized that in two years the sum of the girls' ages will increase by 4. So, now the sum is $15 - 4 = 11$. Since Dana is one year younger than Maya, Dana is 5 and Maya is 6.   ■

Problem 6.37. The sum of the ages of the three kids in a family is 21. In how many years will the sum of their ages be 30?

Most students very quickly figured out that since each year every child gets older by one year, the sum of their ages increases by 3. To finish the problem one needs to compute in how many years the sum of the ages increases by $30 - 21 = 9$ years. It will happen in three years: $9 \div 3 = 3$.   ■

Problem 6.38. Sam and Tom had the same number of marbles. Sam gave three to Tom. How many more marbles than Sam does Tom have now?

Many students insisted that they need to know how many marbles Sam and Tom had originally. Even though we reiterated that this information is excessive, several kids proceeded to solve the problem for a particular case. For example, some assumed that initially Sam and Tom had 10 marbles each and found the answer 6 for that case.

We inquired, "What would happen if the initial amount of marbles Tom and Sam had was not 10?" The kids claimed the answer would be the same. "Why?" A couple of kids needed manipulatives to work it out. In a few minutes everyone was convinced that each time Sam gives a marble to Tom, the difference in the amount of their marbles increases by 2. The children explained it by breaking Sam's action into two steps. First, a marble is taken from Sam, which increases the difference by 1. Then, this marble is given to Tom. Again, the difference increases by 1. Hence, if Sam gave Tom three marbles, the difference would become $3 \times 2 = 6$ marbles.   ∎

Problem 6.39. A princess and an ogre picked the same number of strawberries. Since the ogre likes strawberries less than the princess, he gave her a few berries. Now the princess has 12 more berries than the ogre. How many berries did the ogre give the princess?

Even though this problem is very similar to the previous one, some of the kids had to think about it for a while. Eventually everyone recalled that each time the ogre gave a strawberry to the princess, the difference in the amount of their berries increased by 2. Hence, the ogre should give the princess $12 \div 2 = 6$ strawberries.   ∎

Teacher ▷ In the next four problems the children solve simple systems of two linear equations with two unknowns without realizing it. We found that sketches and colored chalk are extremely helpful for solving these problems.

Problem 6.40. There are rabbits and hens in a cage. I counted five heads and 14 legs. How many rabbits are in the cage?

The majority of our younger students solved this problem by trial and error. We inquired, "What if there were 25 heads and 62 legs?" Hint: "Come up with a method that works for the original problem as well as for the problem with bigger numbers." A couple of kids needed an additional hint: "What if there were only hens in the cage?"

The children explained that if all five heads belonged to hens, there would be 10 legs. We drew the following cartoon on the board to illustrate this case:

The children laughed at the hens we drew but we pointed out that they have everything we care about: the right number of heads and legs.

Since there should be four more legs, the students suggested turning one of the hens into a rabbit. Such a transformation doesn't change the number of heads but adds two legs to the total leg count. To get four additional legs one should perform $4 \div 2 = 2$ such transformations. So, there were two rabbits and three hens in the cage as shown in the picture below. We used colored chalk to add legs to the hens on the board, and the children named this approach a "magic chalk" method.

Several children got the same answer starting with all animals being rabbits and turning some of them into hens by erasing extra legs. ■

Problem 6.41. Six figures, triangles and squares, have 22 edges. How many triangles and how many squares are there? What if there were 17 edges?

Many students remembered the "magic chalk" method we used in the previous problem and applied it here. If all six figures were triangles, there would be $6 \times 3 = 18$ edges. If a triangle is transformed into a square using the "magic chalk", the total number of figures doesn't change but the number of edges increases by 1. Since we need $22 - 18 = 4$ more edges, four triangles should be transformed into squares. Therefore, there are two triangles and four squares.

The kids quickly figured out that six figures (triangles and squares) cannot have 17 edges. They explained that the smallest number of edges is attained when all the figures are triangles. Even in this case there should be 18 edges. ■

Problem 6.42. At a birthday party 30 kids were offered an unlimited amount of ice cream. The reckless ones ate eight servings each, and the cautious ate three servings each. Together the children consumed 115 portions. The next day all cautious kids went to school and the reckless ones stayed at home with stomach aches and sore throats. How many kids, who attended the party, missed school?

Since we gave this problem a few weeks after the previous two problems, many students started by trying to guess the answer and had to rediscover the more efficient "magic chalk" approach.

If all 30 kids at the party were cautious they would have consumed $30 \times 3 = 90$ servings of ice cream. Since 115 portions were eaten, some of the kids were reckless. Using the "magic chalk" one can turn a cautious kid into a reckless one. This transformation increases the number of consumed portions by 5. In order to increase the number of consumed portions by

$115 - 90 = 25$, we need to transform $25 \div 5 = 5$ cautious children into reckless. Thus, there were five reckless kids who missed school.   ∎

Problem 6.43. A king has fauns (who have two legs and two horns) and unicorns (who have four legs and only one horn). Together these animals have 24 legs and 15 horns. How many fauns and how many unicorns does the king have?

Everyone decided to use the "magic chalk" approach. However, this trick didn't work without alternations since when one animal turns into another, both the number of legs and horns changes.

The students decided to draw unicorns and fauns behind a fence so that only horns and hooves were visible. Several children chose to keep the right amount of legs and began by having only unicorns (see the picture below). To get 24 legs, there should be six unicorns. However, six unicorns have only six horns, which is nine horns too few. The children discovered that if one unicorn is turned into a faun using the "magic chalk", the number of legs would change. They proposed to transform one unicorn into two fauns to preserve the number of legs. This transformation increases the total number of horns by three. So there should be $9 \div 3 = 3$ such transformations, which leads to the answer, six fauns and three unicorns.

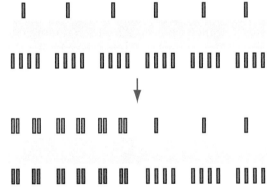

A group of students had a lot of fun coming up with a new animal, "doublefaun", that has four legs and four horns. They transformed three unicorns into "doublefauns" and then replaced each "doublefaun" by two fauns.

Other students used the same approach but preserved the correct number of horns instead of legs. They started with 15 unicorns who have 60 legs. This is 36 legs too many. Two unicorns can be turned into a faun without changing the number of horns. Each such transformation decreases the number of legs by six. So, there should be $36 \div 6 = 6$ transformations. Hence, the are six fauns and $15 - 2 \times 6 = 3$ unicorns.

There is a shorter solution: a faun has the same number of legs and horns, and a unicorn has three legs more than horns. Therefore the excess of $24 - 15 = 9$ legs over the horns must come from three unicorns, and the remaining 12 horns from six fauns. Unfortunately, we never heard it from our kids.   ∎

Teacher ▸ The next three problems deal with parts and the whole. Only the first two of these problems can be solved by children unfamiliar with fractions and multiplication.

Problem 6.44. A full bucket of water weighs 12 lbs. If the same bucket is half full, it weighs 7 lbs. What is the weight of the empty bucket?

The students solved this problem in two different ways:

(1) The difference between the weights of a full and a half-full bucket, $12 - 7 = 5$ lbs, is the weight of the water in the half-full bucket. That means that the bucket itself weighs $7 - 5 = 2$ lbs.

(2) Doubling the weight of a half-full bucket gives the weight of a full bucket and an empty bucket. Then, $2 \times 7 - 12 = 2$ lbs is the weight of the empty bucket.   ∎

Problem 6.45. A book costs $10 plus $\frac{1}{2}$ of its price. How much does the book cost?

Initially many students thought that a half of the book's price is $5. When they realized that in this case the book's price is $10 + $5 = $15 and hence a half of its price is $7\frac{1}{2} \neq $5, they decided that the problem is impossible to solve. Hint: "Make a sketch of the problem statement." Once the children came up with the picture similar to the one below, they quickly finished the problem. A half of the book costs $10, so the entire book costs $20.

BOOK

"1/2"	$10

∎

Problem 6.46. A book costs $6 plus one third of its total cost. How much does the book cost?

Even after solving the previous problem a number of students struggled with this one. They thought that one third of the book costs $2. Drawing a book and marking one third of it helped them to visualize the solution.

BOOK

"1/3"	$6

The total cost is $6 and one third of the total, therefore $6 must be $\frac{2}{3}$ of the cost and the total is $9.   ∎

Teacher ▸ The next three problems introduce the idea of rate. The usual methods of solving rate problems that involve reciprocals (inverse rates) cannot be used with our students. Again, sketches help the children to solve these problems.

Problem 6.47. Three cats take three minutes to eat three cans of food. How long will it take six cats to eat six cans if all the cats eat with the same rate?

We got an immediate incorrect answer: "Six!" In a few minutes many students realized that if three cats eat three cans in three minutes, then each cat finishes one can in three minutes. If the number of cats and cans is doubled, each cat still eats just one can. So, it takes only three minutes.

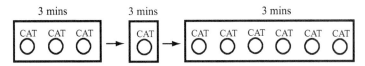

Other kids found the same answer by splitting six cats into two groups of three cats each. Each group finishes three cans in three minutes, so together these six cats finish six cans in three minutes.   ■

Problem 6.48. Sasha and her dad need to paint a room. Working alone, Sasha can finish the job in six hours, and her dad in three hours. How long would it take them to paint this room together?

A couple of kids decided that the answer is 9 hours. We pointed out that working together Sasha and her dad should finish faster than each of them alone, which means that the correct answer should be less than three hours.

Most of our students reasoned that while Sasha is painting a room her dad can paint two rooms. So, in six hours they could paint three rooms. This means that they need only $6 \div 3 = 2$ hours to paint one room.

Several older kids solved this problem using fractions. Since Sasha is working twice slower than her dad, she will paint only a third of a room while her dad paints the remaining $\frac{2}{3}$. That will take $6 \div 3 = 2$ hours.   ■

Problem 6.49. Pooh and Piglet found a pot with 40 ounces of honey. If Piglet ate it alone, it would take him 40 minutes to finish the whole pot. Pooh eats three times faster than Piglet. How long will it take both of them to finish the pot?

The children came up with three different approaches to this problem:

(1) In 40 minutes Piglet would eat one pot of honey while Pooh would eat three such pots. So, together they would eat four pots in 40 minutes. Hence, they will finish the pot in $40 \div 4 = 10$ minutes.

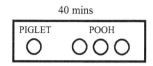

(2) Piglet eats $40 \div 40 = 1$ oz of honey per minute and Pooh eats $3 \times 1 = 3$ oz of honey per minute. Together they eat 4 oz of honey per minute, and it will take them $40 \div 4 = 10$ minutes to eat the full pot.

(3) Since Pooh eats three times faster than Piglet, Piglet will eat $\frac{1}{4}$ of the honey while Pooh eats $\frac{3}{4}$. Since $\frac{1}{4} \times 40 = 10$, the answer is 10 minutes. ■

Teacher The next five problems should be solved going backwards, starting with the final result, and working back one step at a time.

Problem 6.50. There were 24 people in two rooms. After five people left the first room and 15 people left the second, an equal number of people remained in the rooms. How many people were in each room initially?

The kids decided to start with computing the number of people remaining in both rooms. Since five people left the first room and 15 people left the second, $24 - 5 - 15 = 4$ people remained in both rooms, and $4 \div 2 = 2$ in each room. There were $2 + 5 = 7$ people initially in the first room, since five people left the first room. Respectively, there were $2 + 15 = 17$ people in the second room initially.

A few kids calculated the number of people in the second room differently: if there were seven people in the first room, the second room had $24 - 7 = 17$ people. ■

Problem 6.51. Peter gave his brother half of his pencils and three more. Now Peter has nine pencils. How many pencils did Peter have originally?

A few students were confused by this problem. Hint: "Sketch the problem representing the original amount of Peter's pencils as a long bar." Then the children came up with the following picture:

"1/2"	3	9

They explained that if Peter's brother returns three pencils, Peter would have $9 + 3 = 12$ pencils. This is half of what he had originally. Thus, originally Peter had $12 \times 2 = 24$ pencils. ■

Problem 6.52. 27 birds sat on three trees. When five birds moved from the first tree to the second, and three birds moved from the second tree to the third, each tree had the same number of birds. How many birds were sitting on each tree at the beginning?

The children immediately perceived that the total number of birds does not change when the birds move from one tree to another. Thus, there were 27 birds on all trees at the end, or $27 \div 3 = 9$ birds on each tree. Now, the kids needed to trace back the birds' movements. It took some time before the youngest students realized that the first tree lost five birds; the second tree gained five birds and lost three, which means it gained two; the third tree gained three birds. So, the first tree originally had $9 + 5 = 14$ birds. The second tree originally had $9 - 5 + 3 = 7$ birds. Finally, the third tree originally had $9 - 3 = 6$ birds.   ■

Problem 6.53. Paris adores apples. Zeus gave him a few to share with Hera, Athena, and Aphrodite.

(1) Paris immediately ate half of the apples.
(2) Then he ate two more.
(3) Then he ate half of the remaining apples.
(4) The rest he divided equally between three goddesses.

Each goddess got one apple. How many apples did Zeus give Paris?

The majority of the children realized that the problem should be tackled from the end but some needed a hint: "Sketch the problem representing the apples as a bar." The children drew the following:

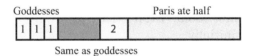

The three apples that Paris gave to the goddesses were a half of what Paris had before step (3). So, he had six apples then. In step (2) Paris ate two apples, so before he had $6 + 2 = 8$ apples. Now, 8 is half of what Paris had initially. Thus, at the beginning Paris had $8 \times 2 = 16$ apples.   ■

Problem 6.54. Again Zeus gave Paris a few apples to share with Hera, Athena, and Aphrodite.

(1) First, Paris ate half of the apples and a half of an apple.
(2) Second, he ate half of the remaining apples and a half of an apple.
(3) Third, he ate half of the remaining apples and a half of an apple.
(4) Finally, he ate half of the remaining apples and a half of an apple.

At the end Paris had no apples left for the goddesses, and each time he ate a whole number of apples. How many apples did Zeus give Paris?

The fastest way to trace this problem backwards proposed by our students included breaking every step into two substeps:

(1a) Paris ate half of the apples.
(1b) He ate one half of an apple.
(2a) He ate half of the remaining apples.
(2b) He ate one half of an apple.

(3a) He ate half of the remaining apples.
(3b) He ate one half of an apple.
(4a) He ate half of the remaining apples.
(4b) He ate one half of an apple.

Reversing substeps (b) the kids added $\frac{1}{2}$ of an apple and reversing substeps (a) they doubled the number of apples. They started at the end with 0 apples:

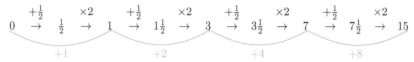

The students commented that Paris ate one, two, four, and eight apples at each step, respectively (shown in green above). He began with 15 apples. ∎

Problem 6.55. Two pens weigh more than three pencils. What is heavier, three pens or four pencils?

The children immediately noticed that a pen is heavier than a pencil. Adding a heavier item to already heavier items (two pens) makes them even heavier than the other set. So, three pens are heavier than four pencils. ∎

Problem 6.56. Winnie the Pooh went to buy pens and pencils. He had just enough money to buy either six pens or 12 pencils. Instead, he spent all his money and bought an equal number of pens and pencils. How many pens and pencils did he buy?

The children determined that each pen costs as much as two pencils, since six pens cost as much as 12 pencils. Most decided to start with having all pens and transform some of them into pencils. Turning one pen into two pencils keeps the total cost of pens and pencils the same. If one pen is transformed, there would be five pens and two pencils. If two pens are transformed, there would be four pens and four pencils. So, Winnie the Pooh bought four pens and four pencils. ∎

Problem 6.57. Three pencils and four pens cost $5.00, while two pencils and two pens cost $2.80. What is the cost of one pencil?

Almost all the children began by drawing a picture similar to the one below.

Then, some students found the answer very quickly while others didn't know how to proceed. Hint: "Can you find the cost of any other combinations of pencils and pens in addition to those already given in the problem?"

Several students decided to double the second combination and found the the cost of four pencils and four pens, $5.60. The difference between this combination and the first combination given in the problem is one pencil, so one pencil costs $0.60.

However, the majority noticed that one can subtract the second combination from the first and compute the cost of one pencil and two pens: $5.00 − $2.80 = $2.20. This new combination and the second combination in the problem statement differ by one pencil. So, subtracting one from the other the kids got the price of one pencil: $2.80 − $2.20 = $0.60. ■

Problem 6.58. Find the largest number such that each of its digits, except the rightmost, is equal to the sum of all the digits to the right.

At first we heard a lot of wrong answers. Some of them, such as 972, didn't fulfill the requirement that each digit is equal to the sum of all the digits to the right: $7 \neq 2$. Other answers, such as 633, satisfied the requirement but weren't the largest. It took the students a few minutes to realize that they should first be looking for the longest possible number that satisfies the requirement and only then for the largest among the longest. Indeed, comparing numbers of different lengths the longest is always the largest. Then, the kids decided to work from right to left. If 1 is put in the ones place, then 1 should be in the tens place too, 2 in the hundreds place, 4 in the thousands place and 8 in the ten thousands place. The kids claimed that 84211 is the largest possible number. We asked, "Why?" and the students explained that if the last digit is greater than 1, the number is at most 4-digits long. For example, if the last digit is 2, the number turns out to be 8422. ■

Teacher ▸ The next three problems are "challenges". They require "outside of the box" unusual ideas. While some children solved them quickly, others thought about them for weeks.

Problem 6.59. You have a rope and a lighter. This rope takes exactly 60 minutes to burn if lighted from one end. However, the thickness of the rope is not uniform, and different parts of the rope may take a different amount of time to burn. How will you measure a period of 30 minutes using this rope?

Now you have two such ropes and a lighter. How will you measure a period of 45 minutes using these ropes?

Several children insisted that the rope should be cut in half. This won't work because each half might burn with different rates. For example, one half may take one minute whereas the other half may take 59 minutes to burn. Other kids suggested lighting the rope in the middle. This method won't work for the same reason. Eventually many children figured out that one should light both ends of the rope simultaneously. Then it will burn twice faster or 30 minutes.

The second part of the problem is much more difficult. Only a few kids came up with the solution: light both ends of one rope and one end of the other rope simultaneously. In 30 minute the first rope will burn down. At that time light the second end of the second rope.   ■

Problem 6.60. Draw a map with four triangular countries such that each country has a common border with the other three. Note that the common border must be a segment.

The students began drawing maps with a lot of enthusiasm, but quickly discovered that the problem is not as easy as they originally thought. Some even claimed it has no answer. After a while several children came up with the following map:

■

Problem 6.61. Make four equilateral triangles using six toothpicks.

This was one of the most challenging problems for our students because it cannot be solved in two dimensions. However, once they realized that the solution is three dimensional, they easily found it: a tetrahedral pyramid has six edges and four triangular faces.

■

Teacher The picture above also shows how to draw a map of four triangular countries on the surface of the globe so that each two have a common border.

Handouts

Pythagoras (570 BCE – 495 BCE)

Pythagoras is often referred to as the first pure mathematician. The exact dates of his birth and death are not known. Various records show that he was born on the island of Samos, Greece, in approximately 569 BCE, and died sometime between 500 BCE and 475 BCE in Metapontum, Italy.

Pythagoras was well educated, he played the lyre throughout his lifetime, knew poetry, and recited Homer. He was interested in mathematics, philosophy, astronomy, and music.

Pythagoras settled in Crotona, a Greek colony in southern Italy, and founded a philosophical and religious school where many of his followers lived and worked. The Pythagoreans' beliefs were based on the power of numbers, honesty, living a simple, unselfish life, and trying to show kindness to people and animals. The followers of Pythagoras were known as *mathematikoi*.

Carl Friedrich Gauss (1777 – 1855)

Carl Friedrich Gauss is sometimes called the "Prince of Mathematics" or the "greatest mathematician since Ancient Greece."

Carl Gauss, a true child prodigy, was born into a poor, uneducated family in Brunswick, Germany, on April 30, 1777. Gauss amazed his parents by learning to add numbers and make calculations before he was able to talk. When he was just three years old, he, supposedly, was already correcting his father's account books. The Duke of Brunswick heard of Gauss's outstanding abilities and gave the 15-year old boy a stipend to study at the university. There, he began making new mathematical discoveries. At 19, he figured out which regular polygons can be constructed using only a ruler and a compass. Gauss was so proud of this discovery that he asked for a regular heptadecagon (a polygon with 17 sides) to be carved on his tombstone.

Gauss did not limit himself to mathematics. He studied magnetism together with the famous physicist, Weber, and discovered a law that was named after him, "Gauss's Law for Magnetism". Gauss also studied optics and came up with a formula for lenses. His most ground-breaking contributions, however, were in the field of mathematics. Even we can understand statements of some of his results. For example, he proved that any whole number can be written as a sum of no more than three triangular numbers. Gauss died in 1855, but we can still encounter his name in many places. A "gauss" is the standard unit of measurement of magnetic influence (induction), named in his honor. There is a moon crater named Gauss, an asteroid christened Gaussia, an Antarctic volcano called Gaussberg, and so on. His portrait used to be on German banknotes before the Euros were introduced.

Leonardo Fibonacci (1170 – 1250)

Leonardo Fibonacci lived about 800 years ago. Nowadays he is best known for the "Fibonacci sequence".

Fibonacci was born around 1170 in Pisa, Italy, into the family of a wealthy merchant, and died around 1250. Fibonacci travelled a lot with his father along the Mediterranean coast and saw how things were done in many European and North African countries. He probably spent much of his youth in the Algerian town of Bougie where his father held an official position.

At that time in Europe, everyone used Roman numerals: I, II, III, IV, V, VI, VII, VIII, IX, X, XI,..., and it was excruciatingly slow to do calculations using them. Meanwhile, the Arabs were using the same system as the one we use now, the Hindu-Arabic numbers.

When Fibonacci returned to Pisa, he decided to introduce Europeans to this better number system, and so he wrote the book "Liber Abaci", which means "Book of the Calculators" (published in 1202). In one of the chapters of "Liber Abaci" Fibonacci described the sequence of numbers now called Fibonacci sequence. This book played an important role in spreading the Hindu-Arabic numeral system throughout Europe.

We only know a little about his life after this. He won a mathematics tournament in 1225 at the court of Pisa. His mathematical achievements were so valued that in 1240 he started to get paid a salary, which was almost unheard of in the Middle Ages!

Blaise Pascal (1623 – 1662)

"Renaissance men" are people who are extremely gifted and successful in many different areas. Blaise Pascal was definitely one of them.

He was a great inventor and a great writer. Even now, 350 years after he died, you can see people reading his books, "Letters" and "Thoughts", in French buses (the bus service was invented by Pascal). He was also a philosopher, mathematician and physicist.

When Pascal was 10, he became interested in the sounds a china plate makes when tapped. Eventually he invented a series of physical experiments that showed that sound is the vibration of air.

Pascal was a sickly child. According to a family legend he was cursed by a witch. His father didn't want to overburden the child, so he didn't allow Pascal to study mathematics. However, the father was forced to change his mind. When Pascal was 12, he discovered on his own the most basic geometric fact about the sum of the angles of a triangle: the sum of the angles in any triangle is always equal to the straight angle, or 180 degrees. (This fact was discovered 2000 years earlier in Ancient Greece.)

Pascal became the first to develop geometry beyond what was known in Ancient Greece. Later he became famous for calculating odds of winning in card games. Among other things, Pascal studied behavior of liquids and air under pressure. The unit of pressure, *pascal*, is named after him.

Pascal constructed the first working mechanical calculator, called the Pascaline. Many other people before him had ideas about how to make mechanical calculators but never succeeded. The Pascaline was built using gears, and could add and substract numbers. Many such calculators were built and sold. Nine of them still exist, and you can find them in museums in France.

Bibliography

[1] A. K. Zvonkin, *Math from Three to Seven*, MSRI, Berkeley, CA, 2011.

[2] D. Fuchs and S. Tabachnikov, *Mathematical omnibus*, American Mathematical Society, Providence, RI, 2007. Thirty lectures on classic mathematics. MR2350979

[3] A. P. Kiselev, *Geometry, Book I. Planimetry,* Adapted from Russian by Alexander Givental, Sumizdat, El Cerrito, CA, 2012.

[4] Natasha Rozhkovskaya, *Math circles for Elementary School Students*, MSRI, Berkeley, CA, 2014.

[5] E. G. Kozlova, *Skazki i Podskazki. Zadachi dlya Matematicheskogo Kruzhka*, MCCME, Moscow, Russia, 2006 (in Russian).

[6] A. V. Spivak, *Matematicheskii Kruzhok*, MCCME, Moscow, Russia, 2010 (in Russian).

[7] A. V. Spivak, *Matematicheskii Prazdnik*, Kvantum, Moscow, Russia, 2004 (in Russian).

[8] T. H. O'Beirne, *Puzzles and paradoxes*: *Fascinating excursions in recreational mathematics; Reprint of the 1965 original,* Dover Publications, Inc., New York, 1984. MR756999

Index